I0045642

Vulnerabilities Position Perspective Opportunities Probability
Rewards Mistakes Situations Momentum

VIII

孫子兵法

Sun Tzu's
Art of War
Playbook
Volume 8 of 9:
Rewards

Gary
Gagliardi

孫子

Sun Tzu's Art of War

Playbook

Volume Eight:
Rewards

by Gary Gagliardi
The Science of Strategy Institute
Clearbridge Publishing

Published by
Science of Strategy Institute, Clearbridge Publishing
 suntzus.com scienceofstrategy.org

First Print Edition
Library of Congress Control Number: 2014909969
Also sold as an ebook under the title Sun Tzu's Warrior Playbook
Copyright 2010, 2011, 2012, 2013, 2014 Gary Gagliardi
ISBN 978-1-929194-83-4(13-digit) 1-929194-83-8 (10-digit)

Originally published as a series of articles on the Science of Strategy Website, scienceofstratregy.org. and
later as an ebook on various sites.

PO Box 33772, Seattle, WA 98133
Phone: (206)542-8947 Fax: (206)546-9756
beckyw@clearbridge.com
garyg@scienceofstrategy.org

Manufactured in the United States of America.
Interior and cover graphic design by Dana and Jeff Wincapaw.
Original Chinese calligraphy by Tsai Yung, Green Dragon Arts, www.greendragonarts.com.

Publisher's Cataloging-in-Publication Data
Sun-tzu, 6th cent. B.C.
Strategy , positioning, success, probability
        [Sun-tzu ping fa, English]
        Art of War Playbook / Sun Tzu and Gary Gagliardi.
        p.197 cm. 23
        Includes introduction to basic competitive philosophy of Sun Tzu

Clearbridge Publishing's books may be purchased for business, for any promotional use,
or for special sales.

Contents

Playbook Overview

Note: This overview is provided for those who have not read the previous volume of Sun Tzu's Art of War Playbook. *It provides an brief overview of the work in general and the general concepts framing the first volume.*

Sun Tzu's **The Art of War** is less a "book" in the modern Western sense than it is an outline for a course of study. Like Euclid's Geometry, simply reading the work teaches us very little. Sun Tzu wrote in in a tradition that expected each line and stanza to be studied in the context of previous statements to build up the foundation for understanding later statements.

To make this work easier for today's readers to understand, we developed the **Strategy Playbook**, the Science of Strategy Institute (SOSI) guidebook to explaining Sun Tzu's strategy in the more familiar format of a series of explanations with examples. These lessons are framed in the context of modern competition rather than ancient military warfare.

This Playbook is the culmination of over a decade of work breaking down Sun Tzu's principles into a series of step-by-step practical articles by the Institute's multiple award-winning author and founder, Gary Gagliardi. The original **Art of War** was written for military generals who understood the philosophical concepts of ancient China, which in itself is a practical hurdle that most modern readers cannot clear. Our **Art of War Playbook** is written for today's reader. It puts Sun Tzu's ideas into everyday, practical language.

The Playbook defines a new science of strategic competition aimed at today's challenges. This science of competition is designed as the complementary opposite of the management science that is taught in most business schools. This science starts, as Sun Tzu did himself, by defining a better, more complete vocabulary for discussing competitive situations. It connects the timeless ideas of Sun Tzu to today's latest thinking in business, mathematics, and psychology.

The entire Playbook consists of two hundred and thirty articles describing over two-thousand interconnected key methods. These articles are organized into nine different areas of strategic skill from understanding positioning to defending vulnerabilities. All together this makes up over a thousand pages of material.

Playbook Access

The Playbook's most up-to-date version is available as separate articles on our website. Live links make it easy to access the connections between various articles and concepts. If you become a SOSI Member, you can access any Playbook article at any time and access their links.

However, at the request of our customers, we also offer these articles as a series of nine eBooks. Each of the nine sections of the entire Playbook makes up a separate eBook, Playbook Parts One Through Nine. These parts flow logically through the Progress Cycle of listen-aim-move-claim (see illustration). Because of the dynamic nature of the on-line version, these eBooks are not going to be as current as the on-line version. You can see a outline of current Playbook articles here and, generally, the eBook version will contain most of the same material in the same order.

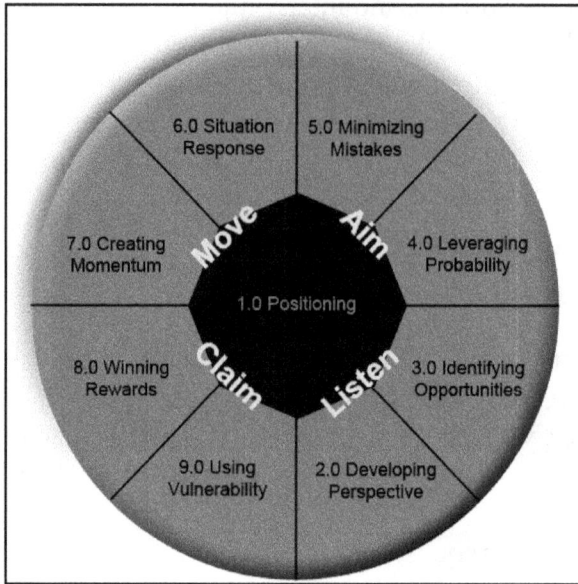

Nine categories of strategic skills define cycle that advances our positions:

1. Comparing Positions,

2. Developing Perspective,

3. Identifying Opportunities,

4. Leveraging Probability,

5. Minimizing Mistakes,

6. Responding To Situations,

7. Creating Momentum,

8. Winning Rewards, And

9. Defending Vulnerabilities.

Playbook Structure and Design

These articles are written in **standard format** including 1) the general principle, 2) the situation, 3) the opportunity, 4) the list of specific Art of War key methods breaking down the general principle into a series of actions, and 5) an illustration of the application of each of those key methods to a specific competitive situation. Key methods are written generically to apply to every competitive arena (business, personal life, career, sports, relationships, etc.) with each specific illustrations drawn from one of these areas.

A number identifies where each article appears in Playbook Structure. For example, the article <u>2.1.3 Strategic Deception</u> is the third article in the first section of the second book in the nine volumes of the Strategy Playbook. In our on-line version, these links are live, clicking on them brings you to the article itself. We provide them because the interconnection of concepts is important in learning Sun Tzu's system.

Playbook Training

Training in Sun Tzu's **warrior skills** does not entail memorizing all these principles. Instead, these concepts are used to develop exercises and tools that allow trainees to put this ideas in practice. While each rule is useful, the heart of Sun Tzu system is the methods that connect all the principles together. Training in these principles is designed to develop a **gut instinct** for how Sun Tzu's strategy is used in different situations to produce success. Principles are interlinked because they describe a comprehensive conceptual **mental model**. Warrior Class training puts trainees in a situation where they must constantly make decisions, rewarding them for making decisions consist with **winning productively instead of destructively**.

About Positions

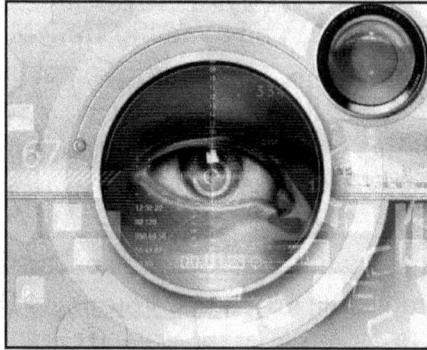

This first volume of Sun Tzu's Playbook focuses on teaching us the nature of strategic positions. "Position awareness" gives you a framework for understanding your strategic situation relative to the conditions around you. It enables you to see your position as part of a larger environment constructed of other positions and the raw elements that create positions. Master Sun Tzu's system of comparing positions, you can understand which aspect of your position are secure and which are the most dynamic and likely to change.

Traditional strategy defines a "position" as a comparison of situations. Game theory defines is as the current decision point that is arrive at as the sum or result of all previous decisions, both yours and those of others. Sun Tzu's methods of positioning awareness are different. They force you to see yourself in the eyes of others. Using these techniques, you broaden your perspective by gathering a range of viewpoints. In a limited sense, the scope of your position defines your area of control within your larger environment. In traditional strategy, five elements--mission, climate, ground, command, and methods--define the dimensions in which competitors can be compared.

Competition as Comparison

Sun Tzu saw that success is based on comparisons. This comparison must take place whenever a choice is made. For Sun Tzu, competition means a comparison of alternative choices or "positions". Battles are won by positioning before they are fought. These positions provide choices for everyone involved. Good positions discourage others from attacking you and invite them to support you. Sun Tzu's system teaches us how to systematically build up our positions to win success in the easiest way possible.

Competing positions are compared on the basis many elements, both objective and subjective. Sun Tzu's strategy is to identify these points of comparison and to understand how to leverage them. Learning Sun Tzu's strategy requires learning the details of how positions are compared and advanced. Sun Tzu taught that fighting to "sort things out" is a foolish way to find learn the strengths and weaknesses of a position. Conflict to tear down opposing positions is the most costly way to win competitive comparisons.

Today's More Competitive World

In the complex, chaotic world of today, we can easily get trapped into destructive rather than productive situations. Even our smallest decisions can have huge impact on our future. The problem is that we are trained for yesterday's world of workers, not today's world of warriors. We are trained in the linear thinking of planning in predictable, hierarchical world. This thinking applies less and less to today's networked, more competitive world.

Following a plan is the worker's skill of working in pre-defined functions in an internal, stable, controlled environment. The competitive strategy of Sun Tzu is the warrior's skill of making good decisions about conditions in complex, fast-changing, competitive environments. Sun Tzu's strategic system teaches us to adapt to the unexpected events that are becoming more and more common in our lives. We live in a world where fewer and fewer key events are planned. Navigating our new world of external challenges requires a different set of skills.

Most of us make our decisions without any understanding of competition. The result is that most of us lose as many battles as we win, never making consistent progress. Events buffet us, turning us in one direction and then the other. Too often, we end up repeating our past patterns of mistakes.

The Science of Strategy Institute teaches you the warrior's skills of adaptive response. There are many organizations that teach planning and organization. The Institute is one of the few places in the world you can get learn competitive thinking, and the only place in the world, with a comprehensive Playbook.

Seeing Situations Differently

Sun Tzu taught that a warrior's decision-making was a matter of reflex. As we develop our strategic decision-making skills, the critical conditions in situations simply "pop" out at us. This isn't magic. The latest research on how decisions are made tells us a lot about why Sun Tzu's principles work. It comes from using patterns to retrain our mind to see conditions differently. The study of successful response arose from military confrontations, where every battle clearly demonstrated how hard it is to predict events in the real world. Sun Tzu saw that winners were always those who knew how to respond appropriately to the dynamic nature of their situation.

Sun Tzu's principles provides a complete model for the key knowledge for understanding conditions in complex dynamic environments. This model "files" each piece of data into the appropriate place in the big picture. As the picture of your situation fills in, you can identify the opportunities hidden within your situation.

Making Decisions about Conditions

Instead of focusing on a series of planned steps, Sun Tzu's principles are about making decisions regarding conditions. It concerns itself with: 1) identifying the relative strengths and weaknesses of competitive positions, 2) advancing positions leveraging opportunities, and 3) the types of responses to specific challenges that work the most frequently. Using Sun Tzu's principles, we call these three areas position awareness , opportunity development , and situation response . Each area that we master broadens your capabilities.

- Position awareness trains us to recognize that competitive situations are defined by the relationship among alternative positions. Developing this perspective never ends. It deepens throughout our lives.
- Opportunity development explores the ground, testing our perceptions. Only testing the edges of perspective through action can we know what is true.
- Situation response trains us to recognize the key characteristics of the immediate situation and to respond appropriately. Only by practice, can we learn to trust the viewpoint we have developed.

Success in competitive environments comes from making better decisions every day. Sharp strategic reflexes flow from a clear understanding of where and when you use which competitive tools methods.

The Key Viewpoints

As an individual, you have a unique and valuable viewpoint, but every viewpoint is inherently limited by its own position. The result is that people cannot get a useful perspective on their own situations and surrounding opportunities. The first formula of positioning awareness involve learning what information is relevant. The most advanced techniques teach how to gather that information and put it into a bigger picture.

Most people see their current situations as the sum of their past successes and failures. Too often people dwell on their mistakes while simultaneously sitting on their laurels. Sun Tzu's strategy forces you to see your position differently. How you arrived at your current position doesn't matter. Your position is what it is. It is shaped by history but history is not destiny.

In this framework, the only thing that matters is where you are going and how you are going to get there. As you begin to develop your strategic reflexes, you start to think more and more about how to secure your current position and advance it.

Seeing the Big Picture

Most people see all the details of their lives, but they cannot see what those detail mean in terms of the big picture. As you master position awareness, you don't see your life as a point but as a path. You see your position in terms of what is changing and what resources are available. You are more aware of your ability to make decisions and your skills in working with others.

Most importantly, this strategic system forces you to get in touch with your core set of goals and values.

Untrained people usually see their life in terms of absolutes: successes and failures, good luck and bad, weakness and strength. As you begin to master position awareness, you begin to see all comparisons of strength and weakness are temporary and relative. A position is not strong or weak in itself. Its strength or weakness depends on how it compares or "fits" with surrounding positions. Weakness and strength are not what a position is, but how you use it.

The Power of Perspective

Positional awareness gives you the specialized vocabulary you need to understanding how situations develop. Mastering this vocabulary, you begin to see the leverage points connecting past and future. You replace vague conceptions of "strength," "momentum," and "innovation" with much more pragmatic definitions that you can actually use on a day to day basis.

Mastering position awareness also changes your relationships with other people. It teaches you a different way of judging truth and character. This methods allow you to spot self-deception and dishonest in others. It also allows you to understand how you can best work with others to compensate for your different weaknesses.

Once you develop a good perspective of position, it naturally leads you to want to learn more about how you can improve you position through the various aspects of opportunity development covered in the subsequent parts of the Strategy Playbook.

Seeing the Invisible

The "Nazca lines" are giant drawings etched across thirty miles of desert on Peru's southern coast. The patterns are only visible at a distance of hundreds of feet in the air. Below that, they look like strange paths or roads to nowhere. Just as we cannot see these lines without the proper perspective, people who master Sun Tzu's methods can suddenly recognize situations that were invisible to them before. Unless we have the right perspective, we cannot compare situations and positions successfully. The most recent scientific research explains why people cannot see these patterns for comparison without developing the network framework of adaptive thinking.[1]

Seeing Patterns

We can imagine patterns in chaotic situations, but seeing real pattern is the difference between success and failure. In our seminars, we demonstrate the power of seeing patterns in a number of exercises.

The mental models used by warrior give them "situation awareness." This situation awareness isn't just vague theory. Recent research shows that it can be measured in a variety of ways.[2] We now know that untrained people fall victim to a flow of confusing information because they don't know where its pieces fit. Those trained in Sun Tzu's mental models plug this stream of information quickly and easily into a bigger picture, transforming the skeleton's provided by Sun Tzu's system into a functioning awareness of your strategic position and its relation to other positions. Each piece of information has a place in that picture. As the information comes in, it fills in the picture, like pieces of a puzzle.

The ability to see the patterns in this bigger picture allows experts in strategy to see what is invisible to most people in a number of ways. They include:

- People trained in Art of War principles--<u>recognition-primed decision-making</u> --see patterns that others do not.
- Trained people can spot anomalies, things that should happen in the network of interactions but don't.
- Trained people are in touch with changes in the environment within appropriate time horizons.
- Trained people recognize complete patterns of interconnected elements under extreme time pressure.

Procedures Make Seeing Difficult

One of the most surprising discoveries from this research is that those who know procedures, that is, a linear view of events, alone have a ***more*** difficult time recognizing patterns than novices. An interesting study[3] examined the different recognition skills of three groups of people 1) experts, 2) novices, and 3) trainers who taught the standard procedures. The three groups were asked to pick out an expert from a group novices in a series of videos showing them performing a decision-making task, in this case, CPR. Experts were able to recognize the expert 90% of the time. Novices recognized the expert 50% of the time. The shocking fact was that trainers performed much worse that the novices, recognizing the expert only 30% of the time.

Why do those who know procedures fail to see what the experts usually see and even novices often see? Because, as research into <u>mental simulations</u> has shown, those with only a procedural model fit everything into that model and ignore elements that don't fit. In the above experiment, interviews with the trainers indicated that they assumed that the experts would always follow the procedural model. In real life, experts adapt to situations where unique conditions often trump procedure. Adapting to the situation rather than following set procedures is a central focus the form of strategy that the Institute teaches.

Missing Expected Elements

People trained to recognize the bigger picture beyond procedures also recognize when expected elements are missing from the picture. These anomalies or, what the cognition experts [4] describe as "negative cues" are invisible to novices *and* to those trained only in procedure. Without sense of the bigger pattern, people are focused too narrowly on the problem at hand. The "dog that didn't bark" from the Sherlock Holmes story, "Silver Blaze," is the most famous example of a negative cue. Only those working from a larger nonprocedural framework can expect certain things to happen and notice when they don't.

The ability to see what is missing also comes from the expectations generated by the mental model. Process-oriented models have the expectation of one step following another, but situation-recognition models create their expectations from signals in the environment. Research [5] into the time horizons of decision-makers shows that different time scales are at work. People at the highest level of organizations must look a year or two down the road, using strategic models that work in that timeframe, doing strategic planning. Decision-makers on the front-lines, however, have to react within minutes or even seconds to changes in their situation, working from their strategic reflexes. The biggest danger is that people get so wrapped up in a process that they lose contact with their environment.

Decisions Under Pressure

Extreme time pressure is what distinguishes front-line decision-making from strategic planners. One of the biggest discoveries in cognitive research [6] is that trained people do much better in seeing their situation instantly and making the correct decisions under time pressure. Researchers found virtually no difference between the decisions that experts made under time pressure when comparing them to decisions made without time pressure. That research also finds that those with less experience and training made dramatically worse decisions when they were put under time pressure.

The central argument for training our strategic reflexes is that our situation results, not from chance or luck, but from <u>the instant decisions</u> that that we all make every day. Our position is the sum of these decisions. If we cannot make the right decisions on the spot, when they are needed, our plans usually come to nothing. This is why we describe training people's strategic reflexes as helping them "do at first what most people only do at last."

The success people experience seeing what is invisible to others is dramatic. To learn more about how the strategic reflexes we teach differ from what can be planned, read about <u>the contrast between planning and reflexes here</u> . As <u>our many members report</u>, the success Sun Tzu's system makes possible is remarkable.

1 Chi, Glaser, & Farr, 1988, The Nature of Expertise, Erlbaum
2 Endsley & Garland, Analysis and Measurement of Situation Awareness
3 Klein & Klein, 1981, "Perceptual/Cognitive Analysis of proficient CPR Performance", Midwestern Psychological Association Meeting, Chicago.
4 Dr. David Noble, Evidence Based Research, Inc.In Gary Klein, Sources of Power, 1999
5 Jacobs & Jaques, 1991, "Executive Leadership".In Gal & Mangelsdofs (eds.), Handbook of Military Psychology, Wiley
6 Calder, Klein, Crandall,1988, "Time Pressure, Skill, and Move Quality in Chess". American Journal of Psychology, 101:481-493

About Winning Rewards

The seven previous volumes of principles explain the principles put you in the position to win success. The focus of the methods in this volume of Sun Tzu's Playbook is proving that your new position succeeds by using it to win rewards.

Positioning for the Payoff

Sun Tzu's strategy deals with the comparisons inherent in competition. The strategic process positions you to be at the right place at the right time. At every step, you learn more about the potential rewards of a situation. The knowledge you acquire is necessary to making a position pay off. However, the process is not yet complete. Without asking for rewards, all your work is wasted. The sad truth is that people are rewarded for providing value to others but only if they claim those rewards. They are rewarded for positioning themselves so that they can win rewards, but the actually winning of awards is its own sub-process.

All competitive positions must generate rewards. Only those rewards give you more resources. Moving to a new position requires using your existing resources. If that move doesn't produce more rewards than it consumes, it isn't profitable. This concept of strategic profit is an innate part of every aspect of Sun Tzu's system.

In a sense, every successful person is a salesperson. Winning rewards is closing the sale. You must sell others on rewarding you. Supporters are always free to choose whether to reward you or not. They choose to reward you for their own reasons. You are at their mercy. In every such competitive choice regarding rewards, their desire for gain battles against their fear of loss. They want to reward you if it helps them. They do not want to reward you if it doesn't help them.

The core of being rewarded is making claims. The ability to make claims connects the value of your position to the needs of others. The claims you make cannot be totally selfish and get rewarded. All claims are based on the Golden Rule—doing for others so that they will do for you. Your values connect you to your supporters. Happy supporters are absolutely necessary for making a position rewarding over the long term.

All rewards, including money, are a by-product of the personal relationships. You follow the other person's lead to win rewards. Winning rewards is like a dance. You must stay in sync with what others are thinking and feeling during the process. When they get ahead of you, you must catch up. When you get ahead of them, you must slow down. You must know how to control the contact without seeming to be in control.

Learn What Specific People Want

You position yourself to win rewards among groups of people. However, Sun Tzu teaches that groups do not make decisions. Only individuals make decisions. You position yourself to influence a group of individuals who can reward you in your competitive arena, but you must win each individual to get the group's support.

Every individual is different. You must learn quickly what individuals care about, that is, what they will reward you for. You must have an interest about their individual desires. You must demonstrate that you care. People don't care about you if you don't first care about them. The faster you learn what individuals need, the faster you can help them decide to reward you.

In making claims, you must become a partner in the process of getting rewarded. You must make it easy for others to reward you. You must know where their interests and desires are. You must avoid getting bogged down in trivialities. You must be knowledgeable about what you offer that deserves rewards, but the real challenge is connecting with people. To do so, you must take advantage of the way they think.

Other people will never believe it if you claim to care about them more than you care about yourself. Nor should you ever believe that people don't care about their own interests. However, you can share goals with others, going back to the ideal of a "shared mission" explored in the first volume of Sun Tzu's Playbook.

Potential supporters *can* believe that you put your long-term goals above your more immediate self-interest. People can also believe that by rewarding you, they can help themselves. Your concern about their individual needs signals whether or not you believe winning their supported by supporting them.

People into Relationships

At first, Sun Tzu's methods for winning rewards can seem contradictory. To win rewards, you must, at some level, forget your desire to win rewards. If people think you are using them, they will abuse you. If people think that you are pushing them, they will push against you. You don't want them to fight you.

To make claims, you must get attention from others, but to get rewarded, you must also pay attention to the people who can reward you. Your claims must communicate with them. Your claims must sometimes be forthright and determined. You must stand up for your belief in the value of what you offer. You must suggest a good process for offering rewards. You must also sometimes be quiet and patient. You must sometimes keep your personal goals to yourself and let others dictate the pace of the process.

If providing value for others is the basis of winning rewards, you can avoid the most common mistakes in making claims. Short-term thinking exaggerates the conflicts inherent among individuals. Long-term thinking allows you to find common ground. Your opportunities come from viewing problems through the eyes of others.

You must also be brave enough to ask for a reward when the time is right. In the end, potential supporters need your help to make a decision. This is another way that you serve yourself by serving them. If you don't make it clear that they have to decide, they won't decide. You leverage the situation by giving them a good reason to decide on rewarding you sooner rather than later.

Your job is to get them excited enough so that addressing your claims is easy. You can approach different people from different directions.

Open-minded people like to hear a variety of reasons to reward you. Get them to agree with any of a list of reasons. Then you can ask them to decide.

For narrow-minded people, you need to find a new reason to reward you. Dangle a novel idea in front of them like bait on a hook. Ask them to reward you based upon seeing the situation from a new angle. This is how you are successful in getting rewarded by narrow-minded customers.

Use Showmanship

You don't claim rewards simple by using words. You talk as little as possible until you understand what people care about. Then, words alone are not enough to get others to see your point. You need pictures, props, and gimmicks.

Demonstrating your value is not nearly enough. Use illustrations and charts. Use showmanship and magic. Use your knowledge to entertain and surprise them. Use the ideas for creating momentum discussed in the previous chapter. You must develop pictures, props, and gimmicks to get people's attention. Make sure customers have the time for you to go through your routine.

You must get your other people's attention. During contact with them, you must use emotion. People only reward others because they feel like rewarding them. The purpose of showmanship is to stimulate their feelings.

People are easily confused about what you want. Keep your presentations asking for recognition short and clear so that they don't frustrate listeners. Make sure that you really understand what their needs and concerns are so that they can understand you needs and concerns. This is how you make people comfortable when you ask them for rewards.

When you ask for a reward, wait for a response. Stay friendly no matter what the answer. Others must offer objections to test the strength of your beliefs. Friendliness, enthusiasm, and patience wear down the people's resistance to rewarding you. It is the same process whether you are asking for a raise or asking for a first kiss. You will be successful if you serve the needs of others. This is how you master persuasion.

Gauging the Value of a Position

If you follow the principles in the first seven volumes of this Playbook, you can put you in a strong position. If you avoid some simple mistakes in acquiring rewards, that position can prove wether or not it is valuable.

First, avoid long drawn-out reward cycles. Like every other part of the campaign, your first rewards should be quick, small, and local. As positions are established, you can build up to larger rewards and longer reward cycles. First, you must prove that your competitive position is valuable winning rewards from others. If you cannot get rewarded, you have chosen the wrong position.

If the initial process is easy and quick and creates happy relationships, your new position will be valuable. Happy relationships lead to more happy relationships and to even more quicker, easier, and more successful rewards. Successful initial claims provide the basis for future claims. Start fast to get rewarded. Take advantage of people's desire to follow others and build on your success. If you generate rewards quickly from new positions, those rewards can quickly pay for the next round of growth and expansion.

The ability to get rewarded arises naturally from good positions if you do nothing to undermine them. Use common sense and do not do anything to create conscious resistance. Do not say anything to threaten firmly held beliefs. Reflect your supporters' interests in everything you do.

Winning rewards is the same both in your business and personal life. It all comes down to creating rewarding relationships from your position. Do not continue to ask for rewards from those who have already agreed to reward you. Do not press the potential supporters too hard for a decision. You must use timing. Avoid asking for attention and decisions when people's minds are busy. Ask for rewards when resistance fades and people want to clarify the relationship so that they can relax and move on. These are the simple principles of customer contact.

How you ask for rewards is the final part, necessary part of your strategy. If you have understood your strengths and weaknesses, chosen the right opportunities, and positioned yourself correctly, you are ready to be rewards. You must know how to ask for rewards at that point. If you think long-term and use showmanship, your rewards are assured.

Some Final Thoughts

You will not be rewarded according to what you deserve. You are rewarded based what you can claim. This means understanding why people reward some claims and not others.

As you read the principles about winning rewards, remember that your goal is to eliminate conflict from the \process. This can seem like a contradiction: you must take a long-term perspective to winning rewards while being rewarded as quickly as possible.

Claiming any rewards—a pay raise, a promotion, a personal favor, or a kiss—is an emotionally demanding process. You must have the right attitude. You must understand the basics of the psychology of persuasion. You must use all the tools of communication and entertainment to make the process emotionally satisfying for your those who you want to reward you.

8.0.0 Winning Rewards

Sun Tzu's seven key methods on how we harvest the rewards of a new position.

> *"Make victory in war pay for itself."*
> Sun Tzu's The Art of War 2:5:1

> *"People often resist change for reasons that make good sense to them, even if those reasons don't correspond to organizational goals. So it is crucial to recognize, reward, and celebrate accomplishments."*
> Rosabeth Moss Kanter

General Principle: Moving to a new position must generate more resources than it consumes.

Situation:

"Advancing a position"doesn't mean simply changing a position. We can easily confuse motion with progress. A sports team can move the ball down the field but unless they score, they don't make progress. Movement isn't progress unless it gets us closer to our goals in a meaningful way. We have a tendency to place too much value in a new position simply because we work to get there. We also have a tendency to continue to invest in non-rewarding positions hoping to turn them around. Sun Tzu's strategy defines success as making victory pay. Winning a new position alone is not success. We must know the methods for turning advances into rewards.

Opportunity:

Our opportunity at this point in the process is to discover the real value of a move. We describe all moves as experiments because we cannot know exactly either the cost or benefits of a new position before attaining it. In the aim step, we select the highest probability opportunities, but a high probability of getting rewarded is far from a guarantee (4.0 Leveraging Probability). After winning a new position, we are in a position to discover what it is worth. If it isn't worth maintaining, it is not worth claiming.

Key Methods:

The following key methods describe how competitive rewards are won.

1. A new position isn't successful unless it gives us additional, tangible resources. We need tangible validation from other people because we have the tendency to overvalue positions. We also have a tendency, called false consensus effect , to over-estimate how much people agree with our assessment. We need other people to give us valuable resources on the basis of our new position to prove its value (8.1 Successful Positions).

2. We must make claims on others in order to get rewards. Positions exist both as facts and opinions. We can do the work necessary to win a new position and create value, but we cannot get rewarded for that work unless we ask others for those rewards. People take conditions for granted. Unless we ask, people may not recognize our work nor think about rewarding us. Only by asking can we start to change the subjective perception of our position (8.2 Making Claims).

3. *To maximize our rewards, we need a clear process that increases our value as perceived by others*. We see and understand the value of our new position, but others are not automatically aware of it, even if its reality is right in front of them. We must know how to gauge, package, engage, and manage that perception of value (8.3 Securing Rewards).

4. *All claims are built on a foundation of individual contact*. Though claims can be made to larger groups, in the end rewards are given by individuals. Individual decisions are affected by the group, but choices are made only by individual. This means that we get rewarded by understanding and following the principles for successful individual contact. Mismanaging contact dramatically decreases our chances of making successful claims (8.4 Individual Support).

5. *To assure action on our rewards, we must know how to leverage people's emotions*. People only take action when they are motivated to do so. That motivation is largely emotional, especially when it comes to winning rewards. The less emotion we generate, the longer it will take to get rewarded. The faster a new position produces tangible rewards, the less our risk and the greater its long-term value is likely to be. The longer a position requires to show its value, the lesser that value is likely to be. It is usually less costly to find a better position than it is to continue to invest in a losing position. Unless we understand and know how to use emotions in our claims, we will never get as much as our position deserves (8.5 Leveraging Emotions).

6. *To claim rewards, we must know how to claim people's attention*. In today's increasingly crowded environment, more and more people are competing for our attention. The chaos of crowded, dynamic environments creates the desire for clarity and simplicity in making claims. We must know how to contrast our claims with the claims of others in order to get attention (8.6 Winning Attention).

7. We must get rewarded in a way that makes future rewards more likely. The"rules of the ground"dictate how claims must be made. Each competitive arena has its own rules. We must know the rules of the ground regarding getting rewarded before we advance to a new position. Learning the rules of the ground is part of the listening stage of strategy, but we set up future rewards by the way we claim our current rewards. At the claim stages, we must conform to those rules to make our new position pay (8.7 Productivity Improvement).

Illustration:

We often compare this process to a prospector staking a claim on a gold mine.

1. A new position isn't successful unless is gives us additional, tangible resources. The process of searching and finding gold isn't enough to get rewarded. A miner who finds gold and doesn't stake and develop his claim correctly has wasted his time.

2. We must make claims on others in order to get rewards. Others must verify that our claim is recorded legally and that the gold is valuable by being willing to buy it.

3. To maximize our rewards, we need a clear process that increases our value as perceived by others. In gold mining, the process is standardized to essaying the gold, staking the claim, filing the claim, and working the mine. Without the process, no formal claim can be made.

4. All claims are built on a foundation of individual contact. We must have others test our goal and legally verify our claim. The testing step is getting the newly discovered ore assayed to see if it is worth mining. The visible claiming step is the same as filing the claim with the government.

5. To maximize our rewards, we must know how to leverage people's emotions. The more excited people about the value of gold, the more likely we are to find investors to help us set up the mine and buyers willing to pay us for the gold.

6. *We must often get the attention of others to get the rewards we deserve*. Gold is a well recognized form of value. Some may not be impressed by it, but most are if we simply make our possession of gold known.

7. *We must get rewarded in a way that makes future rewards more likely*. There are many ways to get rewarded from a gold mine. We could mine it ourselves and sell the gold or we could sell the claim. We must choose the methods that are mostly likely to maximize our return over time. **PDF Download :** Article PDF: 8.0 Winning Rewards

8.1.0 Successful Positions

Sun Tzu's seven key methods on how we harvest the rewards of a new position.

"Make victory in war pay for itself."
Sun Tzu's The Art of War 2:5:1

*"People often resist change for reasons that make good
sense to them, even if those reasons don't correspond
to organizational goals. So it is crucial to recognize,
reward, and celebrate accomplishments."*
Rosabeth Moss Kanter

General Principle: Moving to a new position must generate more resources than it consumes.

Situation:

"Advancing a position"doesn't mean simply changing a position. We can easily confuse motion with progress. A sports team can move the ball down the field but unless they score, they don't make progress. Movement isn't progress unless it gets us closer to our goals in a meaningful way. We have a tendency to place too much value in a new position simply because we work to get there. We also have a tendency to continue to invest in non-rewarding positions hoping to turn them around. Sun Tzu's strategy defines success as making victory pay. Winning a new position alone is not success. We must know the principles for turning advances into rewards.

Opportunity:

Our opportunity at this point in the process is to discover the real value of a move. We describe all moves as experiments because we cannot know exactly either the cost or benefits of a new position before attaining it. In the aim step, we select the highest probability opportunities, but a high probability of getting rewarded is far from a guarantee (4.0 Leveraging Probability). After winning a new position, we are in a position to discover what it is worth. If it isn't worth maintaining, it is not worth claiming.

Key Methods:

The following key methods describe how competitive rewards are won.

1. A new position isn't successful unless it gives us additional, tangible resources. We need tangible validation from other people because we have the tendency to overvalue positions. We also have a tendency, called <u>false consensus effect</u> , to over-estimate how much people agree with our assessment. We need other people to give us valuable resources on the basis of our new position to prove its value (<u>8.1 Successful Positions</u>).

2. We must make claims on others in order to get rewards. Positions exist both as facts and opinions. We can do the work necessary to win a new position and create value, but we cannot get rewarded for that work unless we ask others for those rewards. People take conditions for granted. Unless we ask, people may not recognize our work nor think about rewarding us. Only by asking can we start to change the subjective perception of our position (8.2 Making Claims).

3. *To maximize our rewards, we need a clear process that increases our value as perceived by others*. We see and understand the value of our new position, but others are not automatically aware of it, even if its reality is right in front of them. We must know how to gauge, package, engage, and manage that perception of value (8.3 Securing Rewards).

4. *All claims are built on a foundation of individual contact*. Though claims can be made to larger groups, in the end rewards are given by individuals. Individual decisions are affected by the group, but choices are made only by individual. This means that we get rewarded by understanding and following the methods for successful individual contact. Mismanaging contact dramatically decreases our chances of making successful claims (8.4 Individual Support).

5. *To assure action on our rewards, we must know how to leverage people's emotions*. People only take action when they are motivated to do so. That motivation is largely emotional, especially when it comes to winning rewards. The less emotion we generate, the longer it will take to get rewarded. The faster a new position produces tangible rewards, the less our risk and the greater its long-term value is likely to be. The longer a position requires to show its value, the lesser that value is likely to be. It is usually less costly to find a better position than it is to continue to invest in a losing position. Unless we understand and know how to use emotions in our claims, we will never get as much as our position deserves (8.5 Leveraging Emotions).

6. *To claim rewards, we must know how to claim people's attention*. In today's increasingly crowded environment, more and more people are competing for our attention. The chaos of crowded, dynamic environments creates the desire for clarity and simplicity in making claims. We must know how to contrast our claims with the claims of others in order to get attention (8.6 Winning Attention).

7. We must get rewarded in a way that makes future rewards more likely. The "rules of the ground" dictate how claims must be made. Each competitive arena has its own rules. We must know the rules of the ground regarding getting rewarded before we advance to a new position. Learning the rules of the ground is part of the listening stage of strategy, but we set up future rewards by the way we claim our current rewards. At the claim stages, we must conform to those rules to make our new position pay (8.7 Productivity Improvement).

Illustration:

We often compare this process to a prospector staking a claim on a gold mine.

1. A new position isn't successful unless is gives us additional, tangible resources. The process of searching and finding gold isn't enough to get rewarded. A miner who finds gold and doesn't stake and develop his claim correctly has wasted his time.

2. We must make claims on others in order to get rewards. Others must verify that our claim is recorded legally and that the gold is valuable by being willing to buy it.

3. To maximize our rewards, we need a clear process that increases our value as perceived by others. In gold mining, the process is standardized to essaying the gold, staking the claim, filing the claim, and working the mine. Without the process, no formal claim can be made.

4. All claims are built on a foundation of individual contact. We must have others test our goal and legally verify our claim. The testing step is getting the newly discovered ore assayed to see if it is worth mining. The visible claiming step is the same as filing the claim with the government.

5. To maximize our rewards, we must know how to leverage people's emotions. The more excited people about the value of gold, the more likely we are to find investors to help us set up the mine and buyers willing to pay us for the gold.

6. *We must often get the attention of others to get the rewards we deserve*. Gold is a well recognized form of value. Some may not be impressed by it, but most are if we simply make our possession of gold known.

7. *We must get rewarded in a way that makes future rewards more likely*. There are many ways to get rewarded from a gold mine. We could mine it ourselves and sell the gold or we could sell the claim. We must choose the methods that are mostly likely to maximize our return over time. **PDF Download :** Article PDF: 8.0 Winning Rewards

8.1.1 Transforming Resources

Sun Tzu's six key methods for converting the intangible value of positions to the resources we need.

"Victory comes from everyone sharing the same goals. Victory comes from finding opportunities in problems."
Sun Tzu's The Art of War 3:5:4-5

"The major reason for setting a goal is for what it makes of you to accomplish it. What it makes of you will always be the far greater value than what you get."
Jim Rohn

General Principle: We must convert positions into needed resources by asking those with whom we share values.

Situation:

Our problem is the wide range of goals and values at work within competition. Value comes from our mission but missions can define many different types of value (1.6.2 Types of Motivations).

These values range from the very physical and concrete to the very abstract and idealistic. However, our world is constructed so that our physical, concrete needs must be met if we are to survive to address abstract and idealistic goals. Sun Tzu's strategy is a process that we can use as long as we have the resources to do so. If we run out of those physical resources, the contest is over.

Opportunity:

Fortunately, even extremely abstract forms of value can be translated into concrete resources as long as those values are shared by others (1.6.1 Shared Mission). When free to do so, people readily exchange resources that they have in abundance for things that they value but cannot get directly, even when those values are quite abstract.

Key Methods:

The key methods for converting the resources that we win into the resources we need are:

1. We must eventually convert advances into tangible resources. We need resources to continue advancing our position. We spend our limited time, effort, and other resources to improve our position. To make our investments worthwhile, our advance must return more resources than it costs. In practical terms, this means that we must know how to convert the value a new or expanded position into more immediately and generally useful forms of value such as money (3.1.2 Strategic Profitability).

2. We translated less tangible resources into more tangible resources through shared missions. Positions that serve completely selfish motives cannot be converted into more fungible forms of value. Others do not reward us for gratifying our selfish desires and emotions. Even beggars have to go to the trouble of making public spectacles of themselves in order to give others the gratification of feeling generous and sensitive by giving to them (1.6.1 Shared Mission).

3. The general rule is that we convert resources by exchanging our less tangible resources for the more tangible resources of others. This is possible because people need both tangible and intangible things. This exchange worked according to the principles of complementary opposites. Give us access to resources that are relatively rare, we must translate those resources into those that are more plentiful. We must see how our strengths and abundances can compliment the weaknesses and needs of others. There are many forms of these conversions (3.5 Strength and Weakness).

4. We must identify and connect with those who share our values, lack our resources, but have the resources that we need. This rule simply combines the previous two in a simple action. This connection creates the potential for an exchange to takes place (1.6.1 Shared Mission).

5. We must communicate the value of the exchange. Those with whom we make contact must understand how what we offer serves our shared mission. This doesn't happen automatically. It must be communicated in terms of a shared mission and the emotion that it generates (8.5 Leveraging Emotions).

6. We must ask for the exchange to take place. Unless we ask, the exchange will not occur. The two previous methods set up the potential and motivation for action, but only our action of asking can trigger the required response (2.3.1 Action and Reaction).

Illustration:

Let us illustrate this idea with an extreme example: how do we convert a very idealistic position, say as a missionary, into tangible rewards?

1. We must eventually convert advances into tangible resources. Mother Teresa could not have continued her mission in India without physical support of others.

2. We translated less tangible resources into more tangible resources through shared missions. Her basis for doing this was the fact that others shared her ideas. If they did not, she could not have converted her position in India into anything.

3. The general rule is that we convert resources by exchanging our less tangible resources for the more tangible resources of others. In this case, she exchanged the highest mission values—those philosophical values that make the world a better place over the long-term for the lowest mission values—the need for money and other tangible supplies such as medicine.

4. We must identify and connect with those who share our values, lack our resources, but have the resources that we need. Mother Teresa was able to indentify people who shared her values and contact them, first in personal meetings, later through larger meetings, and finally through large campaigns.

5. We must communicate the value of the exchange. Mother Teresa communicate the concept of her work, helping people die with dignity, and its value to the world to those who were most likely to here and appreciate that message.

6. We must ask for the exchange to take place. Mother Teresa asked people to help according to the basic principles of"ask and you shall receive"and she was not disappointed. People not only gave the physical resources she needed, but gave of themselves, joining her mission.

8.1.2 Reward Boundaries

Sun Tzu's six key methods defining the limits of our control over a position and its rewards.

"You can fail to understand your position and meet opponents.
Then you will fail."

Sun Tzu's The Art of War 10:3:8

"Well, everyone will come to that conclusion sooner or later; for there is a limit to the capacity of man to control events. You may call it Destiny. Another may call it Providence; and a third, God. Names do not matter. It

is the humility that matters; the wonder and the sense of awe that matters."

Atharva Veda

General Principle: Each new advance requires us to discover a new sets of boundaries.

Situation:

Successful moves often lead to tragedy instead of rewards. Since we naturally compare a new position to other positions, especially our past position, the most successful our advance, the more difficulty we have in understanding those limits (1.3.1 Competitive Comparison). The further we come in a short period of time, the more likely we are to misunderstand the boundaries on any strategic position. Political and military history consists of many examples of this problem, called hubris by the ancient Greeks. Modern popstars and especially lottery winners also provide a wealth cautionary examples.

Opportunity:

The boundary conditions on any position represents our span of control. A good understanding of the basic principles of strategy force us to realize that, no matter how great our resources, they are always limited (3.1.1 Resource Limitations). The most critical strategic resource is always information. Despite a flood of information, our information too is always limited (2.1.1 Information Limits). Just as the wealth of information in the modern world has the"haystack effect"of making critical information harder to find, a wealth of resources of all kinds can be finding our limits more difficult. The challenge of too much information in a world flooded with communicationis is so serious that the Institute offers a whole series of free, public articles about it.

Key Methods:

The following key methods explain how we must respect our limits in order to get rewarded.

1. All positions are defined primarily by their limits. It doesn't matter how far we advance our position. It doesn't matter how high we rise within an organization. It doesn't matter how much better our position is relative to the position of others around us. Our span of control is always limited (1.9.2 Span of Control).

2. When one limit is removed, another previously hidden limit takes its place. We advance our position to remove a limit, but when one constraint is removed, there is always another. Influence and control flows through our position like water through a series of pipes with different capacities. When we expand the most constrained point, there is still a constraint somewhere in the system. That constraint only appears after the greater restraint is removed, so the destruction of one limit naturally seems to create another in its place (1.8.1 Creation and Destruction).

3. As we complete a move, we must gather information to quickly assess our limits. Understanding we have limits is different from know what those limits are. We can make mistakes both ways by either missing real limits or imagining false ones. The larger our advance, the less we know about our limits and the harder we must work at understanding those limits (2.2 Information Gathering).

4. Learning about limits requires extending our contact network. All aspects of Sun Tzu's system are loops. In this case, the final claiming step of the Progress Cycle require us to go back to the first step. We need to turn to others to get perspective on our limits. In new positions, we must contact others who are more familiar with the territory than we are. New positions often required building entirely new networks (2.4 Contact Networks).

5. It is safer to underestimate rather than over estimate our control. Underestimating our control means we cannot maximize our rewards, but overestimating our control can result in losing control. No matter how plentiful our resources seem, we are always relatively powerless compared to the large environment. When we rise to positions of "power," others may think that we control conditions, but we do not. We are usually better off limiting our own and other people's expectations about what we can control (5.0 Minimizing Mistakes).

6. Increasing our control in one area often descreases our control in another. This is a natural result of our position existing at a balancing point of complementary opposites. We must adapt to the shift of these forces as we enter a new position, which will offer us a new set of opportunities and a new set of problems (3.2.3 Complementary Opposites).

Illustration:

Whenever we get our heart's desire, we discover that it comes with a new set of limits, but let us illistrate with getting promoted to take over our bosses job.

1. All positions are defined primarily by their limits. Before our promotion, we likely over-estimated what our boss could and couldn't decide, such as how much employees are paid.

2. When one limit is removed, another previously hidden limit takes its place. As boss, we can theoretically set any pay we want for our people, but we are constrained by the need to be profitable. If we lose money, we won't keep our job. If we raise the pay of one person, we likely have to adjust the pay of everyone. We do not discover all these complications until we take over the job.

3. As we complete a move, we must gather information to quickly assess our limits. As a new boss, we cannot exceed our authority but must live up to our responsibilities. We cannot afford to make decisions outside of our span of control because such decisions cannot be executed and we end up stepping on others' toes. However, we must make the ones we are responsible for making.

4. Learning about limits requires extending our contact network. We should ask both our former boss and new superiors about our limits to our responsibilty and authority. However, as Sun Tzu teaches, this isn't enough. We must learn about our authority and responsibility for a broad array of people who see our situation from a perspective that our superiors cannot.

5. It is safer to underestimate rather than over estimate our control. As a boss, when we violate our boundaries of authority, the effects in damaging relationships are going to be more damaging and long-lasting that failing to initially recognize all our responsibilities.

6. Increasing our control in one area often descreases our control in another. As a boss, we have more ability to give other people orders, but we usually get less accurate and timely information as our employees tend to filter the information that gets to us.

8.1.3 Reward Timing

Sun Tzu's six key methods for identifying rewarding positions based upon timing.

"Mastering speed is the essence of war."
Sun Tzu's The Art of War 11:2:16

"Being rich is having money; being wealthy is having time."

Margaret Bonnano

General Principle: The benefits of a position are judged by the relative frequency and consistency of positive events.

Situation:

The advantages of new positions come in a variety of flavors. The problem is that we can only judge the value of new positions once we have moved into them, not before (3.1.5 Unpredictable Value). We cannot know if we have actually improved our position until it proves to be more rewarding than our previous position (1.3.1 Competitive Comparison). Some forms of rewards, especially financial rewards, are quantifiable and theoretically easy to compare, but most of us don't keep detailed ledgers. We keep mental ledgers that record a wide variety of things. Other forms of rewards, such as our level of pleasure, are difficult to compare because they are measure in quality of the experience rather than a comparable quantity. Most situations are a trade-off between quantitative and qualitative values.

Opportunity:

People actually do keep a mental ledger balancing the costs and benefits of things. This quantitative measure works generically for all types of value. It affects every form of advantage and benefit generated by a new position. It is the relative frequency of positive and negative events. This positive and negative feedback is what registers on our mental ledger and it measures in terms of speed and timing. Time passes at a regular, measurable rate for every type and form of position. While rewards must be compared in other ways as well, the consistency of time offers a standard yardstick for comparing the value of any new position to any old position (8.1.1 Transforming Resources).

Key Methods:

Six key methods for evaluating the profitability of a position based on speed and quickness.

1. The key to using time to evaluating new positions is thinking about events. Events can be either positive, negative, or neutral. In using time, we can think about the"reward"as any positive event and the "cost" as the number of other events it takes to get to that positive event (5.1.1 Event Pressure).

2. *Profitability must always be tied to a time period*. New positions are more advantageous if they are more profitable than old positions. While time represents just one dimension, it affects the profitability of a position in a variety of ways. We can think generically about the balance of positive events against negative ones as the ***profitability*** of a position (3.1.2 Strategic Profitability),

3. *More profitable positions create positive events more quickly after our investment than less profitable positions*. This is an issue of quickness in an environment in which opportunity windows close quickly. A new position is more advantageous than a previous position only if its positive events occur more closely to our investments creating those events (5.3.2 Opportunity Window).

4. *More profitable positions create positive events at a faster rate than less profitable positions*. This is simply a matter of the volume of positive results a new position creates. A new position is more advantageous than a previous position only if it generates more positive events in the same amount of time (5.3.1 Speed and Quickness).

5. *More profitable positions create positive events with a greater frequency relative to negative events than less profitable positions*. All positions have both costs and benefits. A position can produce more positive events but also produce more negative ones as well. The issue is the balance between the two. A new position is more advantageous than a previous position only if generates a more positive balance of rewarding and costly events (8.1 Successful Positions).

6. *More profitable positions create positive events more regularly and consistently than less profitable positions*. Consistency creates expectations that people can depend upon. Inconsistent rewards are less valuable than more dependable ones. A new position is more advantageous than a previous position only if its generates positive events more predictably ([7.2.2 Preparing Expectations](#)).

Illustration:

The point of these very generic principles is that they work for a wide variety of competitive situations, where the focus on specific types of rewards do not.

1. The key to using time to evaluating new positions is thinking about events. The value of this system is that a"positive event"can apply to virtually every type of position and every type of value, even when that value is not quantifiable in other ways. It doesn't matter if we are talking about a romantic relationship, a sales call, or a shopping trip, we can say whether the event was positive or not.

2. Profitability must always be tied to a time period. As my Inc. 500 software company grew, we needed a guideline for evaluating new software development projects. We developed the goal of making the new product salable within 90 days. I notice that a similar yardstick is now used by the YCombinator , a seed-stage fund for software start-ups.

3. More profitable positions create positive events more quickly after our investment than less profitable positions. In many situations, there is gap in a time between the investment event and any positive result. For example, we can try to contact someone a long time before actually getting in touch with them. The closer these two events are in time, the better our position. For example, people call back their bosses faster than they call back their subordinates.

4. More profitable positions create positive events at a faster rate than less profitable positions. In making sales calls, contacts can have a positive result in terms of moving the sale forward even when it doesn't generate a sale. We have improved our position if we improve our contact to positive result ratio.

5. *More profitable positions create positive events with a greater frequency relative to negative events than less profitable positions*. A store can offer the best prices more frequently, but those prices can be negated if shopping trips fail to find the products we want, involve poor service, and where policies such as the ability to get refunds add additional costs. Though we cannot keep track of the dollars involved, we can keep track of the balance of events.

6. *More profitable positions create positive events more regularly and consistently than less profitable positions*. In a romantic relationship, contacts that are more consistently and predictably positive represent an advance in the relationship.

8.2.0 Making Claims

Sun Tzu's five key methods for claiming rewards after winning positions.

"Take the enemy's strength from him by stealing away his money."

Sun Tzu's The Art of War 2:4:7

"You are important enough to ask and you are blessed enough to receive back."

Wayne Dyer

General Principle: We must make our claims legitimately to get rewards.

Situation:

Many hard -working, creative, productive people never get rewarded because they fail to make appropriate claims. Some people are rewarded more for their efforts than others. This is not because the people with whom they deal are evil. It is only because the people with whom they deal are human. Benefits and rewards do not naturally flow from even the most advantageous position. If we want to get rewarded, we must understand what a claim is and why it is required to make claims in order to get rewarded.

Opportunity:

In life, we don't get what we deserve. We get what we can successfully claim. What are we really positioning ourselves for through the use of strategy? We are positioning ourselves for making a successful claim. As a psychological and practical matter, we must make claims in order to get rewarded. Rewards are the only proof that what we are doing has value, and we will only get those rewards if we make claims.

Claiming is a responsibility that we only learn as adults. As children, we do not have to make claims. As babies, we cry to get attention. When we are children, our parents pay attention to us because it is their responsibility to do so. It is up to our parents to figure out what we need. When we become adults, we can ask for attention but we won't get it without a reason. It is no one's responsibility to figure out what we need. As children, our parents take care of us. As adults, those with authority over us do not take care of us without giving them a reason. As children, our audience always applauds when we take a bow. As adults, there is always a risk in taking a bow: the silence can be deafening.

Key Methods:

Five key methods describe why claims must be made and what they accomplish in terms of positions.

1. A claim is an outward, visible sign that gains us a benefit or reward from changing our position. Claiming is required both to get our position recognized and to win rewards from a position. Staking a claim is a process, requiring several components (8.3 Securing Rewards).

2. We can only make a claim based upon an external comparison of our position with others. Competition is about being compared to others by others. Like all strategic measures, this is a relative comparison. We must set up comparisons that give us an advantage rather than set us up for failure. We choose our battles, setting up the basis for comparison. This means that we must pick the right group of people with whom we wish to compare ourselves in order to justify our claims. We obviously must pick a group with which we compare relatively well, but it is surprising how often people do the opposite, at least in their minds, making claims impossible (1.3.1 Competitive Comparison).

3. The most important aspect of this process is internal. We must believe our position as valuable to others. We cannot confuse our position with our personality or our ego. Strategically, we think only about position so we can distance our emotional issues from the strategic situation. We must believe that our position deserves a reward before we can claim a reward. (1.0 Strategic Positioning).

4. An objective move to a new position has no meaning until it is subjectively recognized by others. While this process starts from the inside, it is only completed by outside recognition of the value of our position. We must see our position as worthy of rewards from the perspective of others before making a claim. If we have an inflated view of ourselves, our claims are doomed. If we cannot measure up to the judgments of others, our claim will fail. Other must look at our position, compare how it has improved relatively to the position of others and see our advance both objectively and subjectively (1.2 Subobjective Positions).

5. We must actively communicate that perception of our position to those who can reward us. Claims are a matter of communication. If our claims are not communicated, there is no claim at all (8.4 Individual Support)

Illustration:

A more subtle example is advancing our position by losing weight.

1. A claim is an outward, visible sign that gains us a benefit or reward from changing our position. Many people struggle with weight loss because they don't approach it as strategic positioning. Even if they physically lose the weight, they fail to make the appropriate claims on their new position. Too often this means that they fall back to their old position, putting the weight back on.

2. We can only make a claim based upon an external comparison of our position with others. No one is ever happy with their weight, mostly because they compare themselves to the wrong people. Teenage girls who weigh 120 pounds compare themselves to skinny models that weigh 90 pounds. Older women compare themselves to teenagers. By comparing themselves to the wrong groups, people set themselves up for a downhill slide. Even if we weigh 400 pounds, we can make progress if we compare our changing position to those of other 400 pound people. Setting the right gauge allows us to feel our progress rather than be frustrated by it.

3. The most important aspect of this process is internal. After, we lose weight, we will still think we are fat unless we **internally** claim a our new position as a thin person, for example, by buying new clothes. If we want to lose weight and keep it off, we must see ourselves differently. We must see ourselves as a person that can control our weight rather as a person who is the victim of it.

4. An objective move to a new position has no meaning until it is subjectively recognized by others. We will continue to think of ourselves as fat if no one recognizes that we have lost weight. Our mental image of ourselves is formed by our encounters with others. We must claim our position. If we demand recognition from others by making an issue about getting complements, we are more committed to maintaining our new position.

5. We must actively communicate that perception of our position to those who can reward us. If we wear clothes that hide our body, we cannot communicate our weight loss. If we don't commit ourselves to keeping the weight off, we will not keep it off.

8.3.0 Securing Rewards

Sun Tzu's five key methods on maximizing the rewards from a position.

"Some military commanders do not know how to adjust their methods.
They can find an advantageous position.
Still, they cannot use their men effectively."
Sun Tzu's The Art of War 8:1:19-21

"Men are rich only as they give. He who gives great service gets great rewards."
Elbert Hubbard

General Principle: There are four components to getting the most value out of a position.

Situation:

To be successful, we must maximize the benefits we get out of every move. Unfortunately, most people do not have any framework for thinking about the process by which we secure rewards. The problem is that the advantages of a new position are not realized simply by occupying it. Understanding that we must claim rewards is not enough. If we do not know how to use our new position in a process of securing rewards, occupying a position can actually be dangerous. Sometimes, the way in which we get the benefits out of our new position are obvious, but the process by which we maximize rewards is often overlooked.

Opportunity:

The Progress Cycle are not only the four ingredients for advancing a position (1.8 Progress Cycle). The adaptive loop of Listen>Aim>Move>Claim is scale-free and self-similar. This means that it is duplicate in each individual part of the process as well as the process as a whole. At each level, it can be repeated again in a similar, but not identical, way. In the case of the claiming process, we have developed a specific set of terms for these four steps to help us remember them, but beneath this special terminology, we can see the LAMC loop at work. We sometimes describe these four components as four spans in a bridge that takes us from where we are to where we want to go. Just a bridge doesn't take us anywhere unless every span is in place, without the claiming process, our progress often fails.

Key Methods:

There are key methods for using the adaptive loop to maximize our rewards.

1. We must __gauge__ the value of our new position. We must recognize that our perspective is different from those whose support we are hoping to gain. We need a comprehensive method for gauging the value of our position from their perspective so we can claim the appropriate benefits (8.3.1 Gauging Value).

2. We must _package_ the value to clarify its perception. We leverage the boundaries of our position to maximize the perception of its value. Objectively a fact is a fact, but subjectively facts are only important in how others related to them. Fuzzy positions are like an unfocused picture. People cannot see the value (8.3.2 Distinctive Packaging).

3. We must _engage_ others to recognize that value. We must communicate value in a way that demands recognition. This take courage. Good packaging make this easier, but in the end, we must demand others to make a decision about the value of our new position. Engagement requires confronting people with the choice and insisting that they make it (8.3.3 Rules of Engagement).

4. We must _manage_ the value to produce needed resources. Finally, we must manage the position to deliver on the expectations that we have created. When people reward us, we live up to our responsibilities by leveraging the value of the position in the ways that we have promised them(8.3.4 Position Production).

5. We must repeat this cycle in small increments to maximize our rewards. Large initial claims are more likely to fail. How much we get in the long-term is often determined by how often we go through this loop. In each cycle, we must balance our fear of loss with our greed for more. As with all adaptive loops, each cycle brings us closer to our goals of maximizing value (5.4 Minimizing Action).

Illustration:

We often use the analogy of a prospector filing a claim on a gold mine to illustrate these concepts very simply.

1. We must _gauge_ the value of our new position. We must get the gold ore assayed to see its true value,

2. We must _package_ the value to clarify its perception. We must get the right location, especially the borders, for our claim.

3. We must __engage__ others to recognize that value. We must file the claim with the appropriate officials.

4. We must __manage__ the value to produce needed resources. We must make the decision of either choosing to sell the claim or operate the gold mine ourselves.

5. We must repeat this cycle in small increments to maximize our rewards. If we choose to sell or mine ourselves, we must go through this process again to maximize the results of our decision.

8.3.1 Gauging Value

Sun Tzu's five key methods on the methods for correctly measuring a position's value.

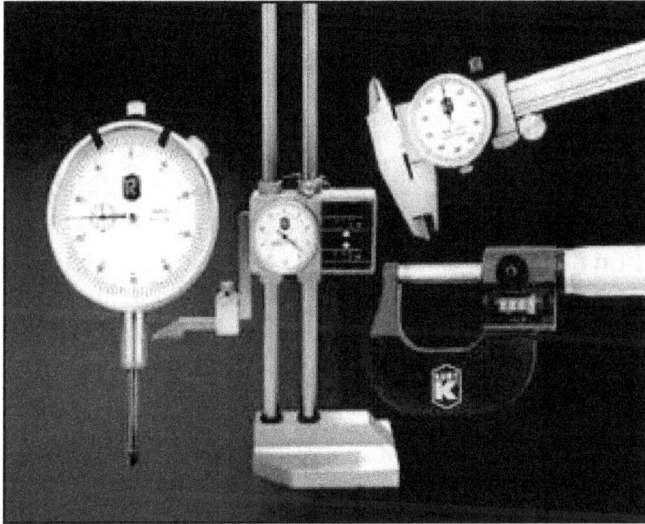

"Some commanders perform this analysis.
If you use these commanders, you will win."
Sun Tzu's The Art of War 1:2:12-13

"The manager has a short-range view; the leader has a
long-range perspective."
Warren G. Bennis

General Principle: There are two key perspectives and five key components in gauging a position's value.

Situation:

To get rewarded, others must recognize the value in supporting us. Their alternatives are either ignoring us or challenging us. We will not get this recognition without the properly gauging the value of our position (8.2 Making Claims). In making claims, we run into two opposite problems with gauging value: the problem of an ego and the problem of insecurity. Our ego tempts us into inflated claims. Our insecurity frightens us away from making any claims. Most people know neither the key elements that make a position valuable nor the role of perspective in gauging the value of a position.

Opportunity:

Gauging the value of a new position involves both objective (physical) and subjective (people's opinions) components of a strategic position (1.2 Subobjective Positions). Our opportunity depends heavily on leveraging what people think, the subjective aspect of this equation (3.6 Leveraging Subjectivity). This is an economic issue. It is less costly to change people's subjective impressions than our physical situation (3.1.2 Strategic Profitability). Even if we physically control a gold mine, its value requires a subjective judgment: the perception of our ownership.

Key Methods:

The following five key methods describe the methods by which we gauge the value of our position to make a claim.

1. Our claims must be both believable and relevant to others. If we make claims that others find unbelievable, they offer us no advantage. If we make claims that no one cares about, we cannot be rewarded. Without making claims from the proper perspective, our claims can hurt us more than they help us. We must test all our claims by both their believability and their relevance (2.3.1 Action and Reaction).

2. We enter the claim stage with most of what we need to know to properly gauge our claims. We learn what we need to know from aiming at an opportunity and completing our moves. During this process, we are continuously gathering information. This information covers all five elements that define our position. The challenge is pulling that information together, filtering it, identifying and highlighting the key points of value (2.5 The Big Picture).

3. We must use our unique,"close up"understanding of the resources and advantages our position offers. We know our position better than anyone else. To make sure that we don't overlook any aspect of value, we must think about all five dimensions that define a position, 1) mission, 2) climate, 3) ground, 4) character, and 5) methods (1.3 Elemental Analysis).

4. We translate our close-up view of value into a perspective that is relevant to those who can reward us. Our potential supporters can be customers, a boss, or even an opponent who we wish to intimidate. What defines them as potential supporters is that we want something from them. This translation process is exactly that: putting one view of value into the terms of another (2.0 Developing Perspective).

5. This translation requires asking five questions about the value of our position to others. 1) How do others share the value of what we see as our mission? 2) How do the changes that concern them increase the value of our position over time? 3) How do the resources from the ground we control benefit others? 4) How do aspects of our character complement their weaknesses and strengths of their character? 5) How do our skills and systems increase the value of their skills and systems? (2.3.4 Using Questions).

Illustration:

Let us look at the challenge of gauging value in getting rewarded for the value of expanding our responsibilities at work.

1. Our claims must be both believable and relevant to others. If we want to get rewarded for the work we are doing, we must make a claim, but that claim cannot be based on our perspective, the effort we put into the work, but from the perspective of our boss and what he rewards people for doing.

2. We enter the claim stage with most of what we need to know to properly gauge our claims. As our responsibilities at work expand, we know what we are doing. We also know our boss and what he cares about.

3. We must use our unique,"close up"understanding of the resources and advantages our position offers. We are close to our jobs, so we know what we are doing and how our role has expanded over time. The person who controls our paycheck never has the same information.

4. We translate our close-up view of value into a perspective that is relevant to those who can reward us. We must put that value into terms that our boss will accept and care about. Sometimes, how he rewards people is a matter of company policy not personal choice. Before making our claim, we must translate what we do into terms of value that our boss can relate to and for which he can compensate us.

5. This translation requires asking five questions about the value of our position to others. How does the additional work we are doing 1) produce more value related to our organization's and boss's goals? 2) affect the changing business conditions that create challenges and opportunities for our organization and boss? 3) generate more resources (income, customers, products, etc.) for the organization? 5) depend on our particular strengths character (creativity, leadership, courage, etc) lacking elsewhere in the organization? and 6) depend on our particular skills (knowledge, experience, contacts, etc) lacking elsewhere in the organization?

8.3.2 Distinctive Packaging

Sun Tzu's nine key methods for creating the perception of value.

"You must master gongs, drums, banners, and flags. Place people as a single unit where they can all see and hear."

Sun Tzu's The Art of War7:4:6-7

"The most important persuasion tool you have in your entire arsenal is integrity."

Zig Ziglar

General Principle: We must package the advantages of our position to maximize the perception of value.

Situation:

Strategically, perception is not reality, but it is a key component of reality (1.2 Subobjective Positions). Our challenge is having people recognize the greatest value of our position. Just because we understand the value of our position doesn't mean that others will. This is particularly a problem when we have recently advanced our position--taken on new responsibilities at work, brought out new products, become more committed to a relationship, etc. The problem is that others always tend to continue to think of us in terms of where we were rather than where we are today.

Opportunity:

When perception and reality separate, reality provides the anchor, and perception provides the energy. As complementary opposites , they create one another in a constant cycle (3.2.3 Complementary Opposites). This means there are real limits to how far apart reality and perception can drift apart. In packaging a new position, we have an opportunity to sharply define the value of our new position from either reality or perception. All four methods for winning rewards from our position requires understanding psychology, but packaging methods use the deepest psychology (8.3 Securing Rewards).

Key Methods:

We use the following nine key methods to sharpen people's perception of the value of our position relying heavily on psychological research.

1. A package must clarify the new boundaries of our position. A fuzzy position is as difficult to appreciate as a fuzzy picture and less valuable. The job of packaging is to bring our position, especially how our limited resources are being better used, into sharp focus (3.1.2 Strategic Profitability).

2. A package must clarify the position's value to others. We want to focus the value of our position from the perspective of the specific people whose estimation determines the rewards of that position. This perspective can only be understood in terms of their values, not ours (3.6 Leveraging Subjectivity).

3. *A package must clarify* how *our position has grown in value*. In clarifying our position, we should show how our boundaries have changed and grown to encompass more value. Strategic comparisons are all relative: comparing one position to another (1.3.1 Competitive Comparison).

4. *The resulting package must not only persuade but correctly set expectations*. If the package, that is, the perception, oversells the position, it creates disappointment in the reality. Thinking longer term, we don't want people to be unhappy after they open the package. Packaging is preparation and practice for the next step, engaging people to recognize and reward the value of our position (7.2.2 Preparing Expectations).

5. *We want to package the value of our new position to others as an agreement*. People want to honor commitment, even if the original incentive or motivation is subsequently removed. The Asch conformity experiments demonstrate that people will act. We should package our new position as honoring our half of an agreement (1.6 Mission Values).

6. *We want to package the value of our new position to others as a Trend*. People will do things that they see other people are doing. We want to package the value of our position with"social proof"of recognition by others. (1.3.1 Competitive Comparison)

7. *We want to package the value of our new position to others as a Rarity*, Scarcity generates demand. We need to highlight the elements of our position that are difficult to find (1.3.2 Element Scalability).

8. *We want to package the value of our new position to others as a Command*. People want to obey authority figures. Milgram experiments in the early 1960s and the My Lai massacre.We should package in any evidence that those in authority have ordered such rewards. (1.5.1 Command Leadership)

9. *We want to package the value of our new position to others as a Favor*. People tend to return favors out of reciprocity but respond poorly to demands. We should package our new position as giving a gift that has not been returned (1.5.2. Group Methods.

Illustration:

Extending the example we used in the article gauging a position's value, packaging for getting rewarded for extending our responsibilities at work (8.3.1 Gauging Value).

1. A package must clarify the new boundaries of our position.
We specifically identify the new responsibilities that we have undertaken, when and why we took those responsibilities.

2. A package must clarify the position's value to others. We translate these responsibilities from the tasks involved to the value that those tasks generate both for our organization and for the specific person with who we are dealing.

3. A package must clarify how our position has grown in value. To sharpen the value of our position, we should specifically contrast what we were doing, what we stopped doing, and how what we are doing now is more valuable.

4. The resulting package must not only persuade but correctly set expectations. We want to package our position in a way that doesn't set expectations that we cannot live up to.

5. We want to package the value of our new position to others as an <u>agreement</u>. We can connect our extension of responsibilities to a pay-raise as part of previous agreement.

6. We want to package the value of our new position to others as a <u>trend</u>. We can demonstrate that others with similar extensions of responsibilities have been similarly rewarded.

7. We want to package the value of our new position to others as a <u>rarity</u>. We can make it clear that those who show such initiative are rare.

8. We want to package the value of our new position to others as a <u>command</u>. We can maintain that rewarding behavior like ours has long been part of company policy.

9. We want to package the value of our new position to others as a _favor_. We can package the work that we have done as a favor that has helped our boss and his position.

8.3.3 Rules of Engagement

Sun Tzu's nine key methods outlining the do's and don't of making claims.

"Victory goes to those who make winning easy. A good battle is one that you will obviously win."
Sun Tzu's The Art of War 4:3:13-14

"The modern nose, like the modern eye, has developed a sort of microscopic, inter-cellular intensity which makes our human contacts painful and revolting."
Marshall McLuhan

General Principle: We must know how to engage people to win recognition of our value.

Situation:

Sun Tzu's strategy requires us to retrain our instincts about how to make decisions about conditions. Our only inborn"strategic"reactions to others are the"flight or fight"response (2.3.3 Range of Reactions). Needless to say, in a society where we can only get rewarded through our contact with other people, these reactions are not very useful.

The problem is that we are increasingly isolated by modern forms of communication. This isolation is a major strategic problem because we cannot get rewarded for advancing our position without engaging \others (8.2 Making Claims), leveraging our position into rewards. Modern communication tools such as Twitter can increase our isolation in an increasingly crowded world when they are used to disengage us from meaningful contact with others.

Opportunity:

Direct human contact is the primary source of all strategic rewards. If we go back a hundred years, its was also the source of all entertainment and diversion. People didn't have to be trained in human contact because their lives revolved around it. The opportunity today is that most of us our relatively unskilled and uncertain in our direct contact with others.

In a sense, all the principles of Sun Tzu teach us how to better conduct human contact. Because so few of us develop the skills of human contact, certain professions--salespeople, politicians, people in the media-enjoy a huge advantage because they have an opportunity to develop these atrophied skills. Skill at contact begins with understanding why we must seek it our in order to be rewarded.

Key Methods:

The following nine key methods explain the best ways to engage others while making a claim.

1. The rules of engaging others apply to every type of contact. The general do's and don'ts for engaging others to claim rewards apply to every kind of meeting from one-to-one meetings, to group meetings, to making public appearances, to sending out emails, and so on. Other Playbook articles deal with the specific methods of working with individuals one-on-one (8.4 Individual Contact).

2. These generic principles of claiming are always trumped by"the rules of the ground". Different competitive arenas--selling a product, proposing marriage, constructing an alliance, winning a football game and so--require that the specific rules of the game be followed. We don't score in a relationship the same way we do in a football game. (2.4.1 Ground Perspective).

3. Do make more frequent and broader contact increase our probability of rewards. We engage people to that, even if they don't reward immediately, we set up another contact where they can (4.0 Leveraging Probability).

4. We must be prepared for personal encounters where we make a claim. Making a claim is a delicate matter and without the proper preparation, it leads only to disaster. If the opportunity for a meeting suddenly appears, we cannot take it unless we know exactly what will work. Making a claim is a delicate matter and without the proper preparation, it leads only to disaster (5.0 Minimizing Mistakes).

5. We should set up special claim encounters outside of the regular course of events. On occasions where people expect claims to be made, claims are also normally rejected. Claim engagement must involve at least an element of surprise and creativity (7.0 Creating Momentum).

6. Our contacts must reinforce the firmly held beliefs of others and the advantages of their position. We cannot use our claim directly challenge the legitimate position of another. Our claims should be consistent with what people believe, especially about their own position (3.1.3 Conflict Cost).

7. Rewarding contacts move quickly and lightly rather than slowly and heavily. A series of quick, small, successful claims is more certain than pushing for a large, significant award (5.4 Minimizing Action).

8. We must work hard to be heard and understood. Others do not necessarily hear what we say. In claim situations, it is totally our job to make sure that we are heard and understood (2.3 Personal Interactions).

9. Our focus must always be on creating a common cause with others. While we look for awards to satisfy our needs, they are only given if we satisfy the needs of others (1.6.1 Shared Mission)

Illustration:

Let us illustrate these ideas with examples from selling.

1. The rules of engaging others apply to every type of contact. When we are selling, we are always selling whether we are making a sales call or making a presentation to the Rotary.

2. Generic principles of rewarding contact are always trumped by"the rules of the ground". Jet planes are not sold in the same way that vacuum cleaners, even if they have many things in common.

3. More frequent and longer contacts increase our probability of rewards. If we want to sell a product or service, the more people that we can contact more often, the more we will sales.

4. We must be prepared for personal encounters where we make a claim. If we run into our prospect when we are unprepared, we should take the opportunity to build the relationship rather than trying to close the sale.

5. We should set up special claim encounters outside of the regular course of events. More sales are closed on the golf course than the board room.

6. *Our contacts must reinforce the firmly held beliefs of others and the advantages of their position.* If we want to close a sale, the least successful method is to pressure people into an immediate decision. Even if it works, it never creates a satisfied, repeat customer.

7. *Rewarding contacts move quickly and lightly rather than slowly and heavily.* For a salesperson, it is always better to make a small sale now that can lead to a sale in the future than try to get a large sale immediately.

8. *We must work hard to be heard and understood.* After we make a statement about the value of a product, it is always best to ask the other prospect for a confirmation of that value in their own words.

9. *Our focus must always be on creating a common cause with others.* In sales, we teach that getting rewarded is not about how great our product is, but how great the product can make our customers.

8.3.4 Position Production

Sun Tzu's seven key methods describing the shift from profitable competition to profitable production.

*"This is how you serve your country.
This is how you reward your nation."*
Sun Tzu's The Art of War 10:3:20-21

"I feel that the greatest reward for doing is the opportunity to do more."
Jonas Salk

General Principle: We must use organizational skills to produce the most value of our position to satisfy expectations.

Situation:

Our success in competition takes us from the competitive arena into the productive one. We may think that the difficult work is behind us after we get others to recognize the value of our position, but it is simply the start of a new task, one which requires very different skills. The problem is that the strategic skills that win positions are different from the production skills that produce value from those positions over time. We cannot maximize our rewards from competition simply from competitive skills. We need productive skills. Many people cannot make the transition. We see this when people on the front lines of competition are promoted to internal management positions.

Opportunity:

Our opportunity is knowing how to make the switch between the warrior skills of competition and the management skills of production. These two skill sets are mirror images of each other. We can dramatically improve our rewards from competition by shifting from competitive thinking to productive thinking. Since we are all trained in school in the methods of linear planning, many competitors can make the transition rather easily, but only if they understand the transition that is involved.

Key Methods:

The following key methods get the most reward from production within our span of control.

1. We must produce the most possible value from our span of control to exceed expectations. After people reward us, we must reward them by living up to our responsibilities. This means knowing how to produce the most value from the positions which we have been recognized to control (1.9.2 Span of Control).

2. Our skills at production are the complementary opposite of our skills of competition. Our success in generating value from our position depends on recognizing the difference between these two realms and switching back and forth from competition to production as appropriate (3.2.3 Complementary Opposites).

3. A productive mission and goals focus on a well-specified end result rather than a general improvement in position. We seek to produce duplicate, standard products rather than unique, custom solutions (1.6 Mission Values).

4. The controlled climate of production consists of predetermined steps rather than unpredictable events. The steps exist within our span of control so they must be planned in advance. We measure predictability to increase our control. As we increase our control, we minimize waste and effort while maximizing quality (1.4.1 Climate Shift).

5. The controlled ground within our span of control is defined by cooperative action and known resources. This is in contrast with the competitive environments where people compete and resources are undetermined and unattained. Since resources are known and available resources, they can be organized (1.4.2 Ground Features).

6. Productive individual decision-making process requires linear thinking and reductionist problem solving. Reductionism breaks processes into smaller parts to identify the location of problems. A competitive environment requires adaptive thinking and holistic problem solving that fit details into larger picture (1.5.1 Command Leadership).

7. Productive group methods require organizing and designing. These methods seek to control a part of the environment rather than adjust to environment as a whole. This is the opposite of competitive methods that are based on exploring and experimenting (1.5.2. Group Methods).

Illustration:

Below are some general examples of the differences between the skills by which positions are won and the skills by which production from a position is maximized.

1. We must produce the most possible value from our span of control to exceed expectations. In our career, we win a promotion by winning recognition in competition with others, but we justify our promotion by living up to our responsibilities. In business, we win customers by promotion and marketing, but we keep customers by providing excellent service and value. In our relationships, we win affection by positioning ourselves as exciting and interesting, but we keep relationships by proving ourselves dependable and consistent. In sports, when a good assistant coach is promoted to a head coach, he or she must make decisions about planning personnel, pay, and organization as well as about game strategy.

2. Our skills at production are the complementary opposite of our skills of competition. In our career, we must know where competition stops. In business, we must satisfy customer expectations. In our relationships, we must become a team. In sports, a coach must assume complete authority.

3. A productive mission and goals focus on a well-specified end result rather than a general improvement in position. In our career, in business, in our relationships, in sports, we must have clear, specific production goals to be successful.

4. The controlled climate of production consists of predetermined steps rather than unpredictable events. In our career, in business, in our relationships, in sports, we must have clear, well-defined processes and measurement to be successful.

5. The controlled ground within our span of control consists is defined by cooperative action and known resources. In our career, in business, in our relationships, in sports, we must control and organize our resources for maximum benefit.

6. Productive individual decision-making process requires linear thinking and reductionist problem solving. In our career, in business, in our relationships, in sports, we must locate and identify the specific location of problems that are holding us back.

7. Productive group methods require organizing and designing. In our career, in business, in our relationships, in sports, we must work as a team, balancing and respecting our different skills for the maximum benefit.

8.4.0 Individual Support

Sun Tzu's eight key methods describing the general techniques for winning the support of individuals.

"An organized force is braver than lone individuals.
This is the art of organization."

Sun Tzu's The Art of War 11:4:18-19

The best way to persuade people is with your ears - by listening to them."

Dean Rusk

General Principle: Our success depends on the individual decisions of others.

Situation:

Rewards usually come down to the decisions of individuals. When a single individual must decide, the average behavior of the crowd no longer matters (1.8.4 Probabilistic Process). Decisions by individuals are different from a group decisions. Individuals are never average. The problem is that strategy teaches us to think in probabilities, but we cannot treat individuals as we do a group. Working with individuals requires its own special methods.

Opportunity:

Working with individuals provides more opportunities to use different strategic methods than working with groups. Both require adapting to the environment, but they differ dramatically in cycle time (1.8.3 Cycle Time). During one-on-one contact, we must adapt from second to second to what the encounter reveals. The more wedded we are to our plans, the less successful we will be. As Sun Tzu indicates in our opening quote, people are naturally afraid to make decisions. If we use the right methods to work with them, we can get the decisions that we want. For this reason, preparation and practice are more important than planning. Quick thinking is more frequently rewarded than well-constructed promotions.

Key Methods:

The following key methods from Sun Tzu regarding individual contact.

1. During individual contact, we must see the situation from the other person's perspective. To get rewarded, we must adapt the special conditions that every individual brings to every decision. Until we know what individuals think, we cannot ask them to make a decision. When making contact with individuals, we must subordinate positioning statements to focus on the specific interests of the individual. We can try to shortcut the contact process. If we do, we will hurt our chances of success (2.0 Developing Perspective).

2. Prepare before the contact but be prepared to adapt during it. When we can know the decision maker before the contact, we must learn all we can about them beforehand but we cannot be surprised if much of what we learn is misleading (2.1.1 Information Limits).

3. Know **the time and place of meetings but take advantage of unexpected meetings**. The best is when we can control the entire setting to our advantage, but if we happen to get on an elevator with a decision-maker, we should be prepared for contact (2.3.2 Reaction Unpredictability).

4. **Ask questions and listen without making assumptions**. We must know the conditions before reacting them. Assuming we know a situation because we know the probabilities is always a mistake. Without the proper information, what we say is as likely to hurt our chances of getting a reward as help it. Conditions that dominate the other person's thinking **are** the dominant conditions (6.2.1 Campaign Flow).

5. **Lead the conversation with questions but respond immediately to what is said**. We can lead with questions but not as as a means of controlling it. We must become the decision maker's partner in the process, making it easy for them to reward us. We use questions as a means of discovering an opening. The key information can come only from the other person (2.6 Knowledge Leverage).

6. **When we want to make a point, we need feedback to get a reaction**. Others do not necessarily hear what we say. In claim situations, it is totally our job to make sure that we are heard and understood by the other person (2.3 Personal Interactions).

7. **Focus everything on creating a common cause with the individual**. While we look for awards to satisfy our needs, they are only given if we satisfy the needs of others. Decision makers will never believe that we care about them personally more than we care about ourselves. Decision makers **can** believe that we are rewarded only by rewarding them (1.6.1 Shared Mission).

8. **The pressure on the individual must arise from positioning and the situation not from us personally**. We cannot pressure individuals into making the decisions that we want. Transparent pressure aimed at an individual weakens our positioning, creating suspicion and doubt. The subtle jujitsu demonstrated by our ability

to adapt to their needs while asking them to meet our needs is more powerful (5.1.1 Event Pressure).

Illustration:

The science of one-on-one contact has been advanced primarily in selling and negotiations. In business, we draw a distinction between marketing, which applies to groups, and selling, which happens between individuals. In business, this transition from the general to the specific is easy to see. We market our products and position our companies in a general way to groups of people. All our sales, however, are made to individuals and, when we rely on a sales force, but individuals. Marketing looks to create a competitive advantages in positioning, but that advantage must translate into a specific sale to win an award. The Institute's most popular book, *The Art of War for the Sales Warrior* directly applies every strategic lesson from Sun Tzu to the challenge of individual contact.

Let us illustrate these key methods from the perspective of a salesperson:

1. During individual contact, we must see the situation from the other person's perspective. Most salespeople make the mistake of representing the interests of their company. They should be representing the interests of their prospects as addressed by their company.

2. Prepare before the contact but be prepared to adapt during it. When working on large, long term corporate sales, we can research the decision maker before the sale, but in retail sales, we must work with whoever walks through the door so our preparation must focus on knowing the product.

3. Know the time and place of meetings but take advantage of unexpected meetings. If we can get potential customers to visit us, we can control the environment to make the sale more easily but every good salesperson should have an"elevator pitch"prepared for chance encounters.

4. *Ask questions and listen without making assumptions*. A good salesperson uses the first step in the sales process, the qualification stage, to search for the customer's"hot buttons"that will determine the decision.

5. *Lead the conversation with questions but respond immediately to what is said*. A good salesperson realizes that it is better to ask than to tell. We prepare questions that lead the conversation in a way that lets the customer tell us they want and what is good about our product.

6. *When we want to make a point, we need feedback to get a reaction*. A salesperson provides the information that the customer needs to make a decision but must check to make sure that the provided information answers the customer's questions, both asked and unasked.

7. *Focus everything on creating a common cause with the individual*. The customer knows that the salesperson is trying to make a sale, but the customer can believe that it is good business to create satisfied customers that come back and bring their friends because it is!

8. *The pressure on the individual must arise from positioning and the situation not from us personally*. Discount deadlines, company policies, limited amount of stock, and so one should provide the pressure to decide. As a salesperson, we should apologize for that pressure while making customers aware of it as a service to them.

8.5.0 Leveraging Emotions

Sun Tzu's eight key methods describing how we use emotion to obtain rewards.

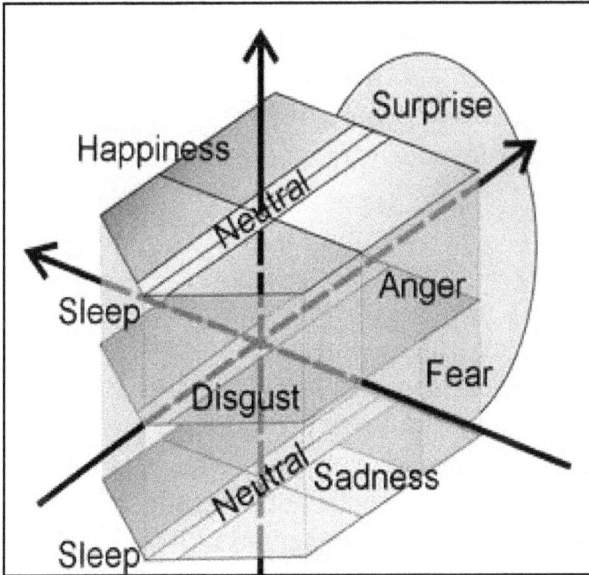

"Offer men safety and they will stay calm.
Endanger them and they will act."
Sun Tzu's The Art of War 5:5:13-14

Let one who wants to move and convince others, first be convinced and moved themselves. If a person speaks with genuine earnestness the thoughts, the emotion and the actual condition of their own heart, others will listen because we all are knit together."
Thomas Carlyle

General Principle: To maximize our rewards, we must leverage the emotion of others.

Situation:

According to Sun Tzu, only emotional energy spurs action. To win rewards, we require action from our supporters. This means that we must trigger emotions in supporters without inflaming the emotions of our opponents. The problem is our own emotions. Uncontrolled, they can either amplify or dampen the emotions of others. Most of us don't think of our emotions as tools to be used. These uncontrolled emotions are as likely to inflame the emotions of our opponents while discouraging the emotions of our supporters. The failure to get rewarded is often the fault of misusing the levers of emotion.

Opportunity:

Our emotions are triggered by actual events and potential events. Actual events trigger happiness or sadness. Potential events trigger hope or fear. Our opportunity to control emotions arises from our understanding of the levers of emotion. These levers include the forces driving change, our control of perceptions, the psychology of groups, and our personal interactions. All of these levers work according to the general principle of complementary opposites. When events go one direction, emotions are amplified or dampened. The perception of potential events is much easier to control than actual events because subjective perceptions of the future are easier to manipulate that physical reality (2.1.2 Leveraging Uncertainty).

Key Methods:

There are eight key methods describing Sun Tzu's principles for using emotion to create action.

1. We must target individuals from whom we want action. These people are either potential supporters that we want to motivate or opponents who are standing in our way (2.3.1 Action and Reaction)

2. We must identify potential future events that create strong emotions in these people. The most common such emotions are the hope for gain and the fear of loss. Of these two, the fear of loss, known as loss aversion , is stronger (2.4.2 Climate Perspective).

3. Individual emotional appeals can be specific. Emotional appeals to individuals can be focused on very specific actions. They can also be more subtle. They are also effective a higher percentage of the time. However, they require more information on our part (8.4 Individual Support).

4. Group emotional appeals can and should be more aggressive. When dealing with crowds, we can use extreme and broad appeals to emotion. The reaction of the crowd will tend to carry the individual along with it. However, group appeals will be less effective overall and tend to fade quickly. (1.5.2. Group Methods).

5. We must use what is known about the past. The past consists of both trends in a certain direction and of cyclical patterns that repeat themselves. We want to demonstrate a trend that can help or hurt them if they fail to act now (2.6 Knowledge Leverage).

6. We must use what is unknown about the future. The future has many different forms of uncertainty. We must select the ones that work to our advantage to illustrate the dangers of the future. The unknown always creates fear. You want to use the fear of loss if they fail to act (2.1.2 Leveraging Uncertainty).

7. We must take the side of those from whom we want action. We can take the side of both potential supporters and existing opponents. To take their side, we must create an opposing force, an"enemy,"that puts us both on the same side. This enemy can be a person or an impersonal force of nature. Since we are taking their side, we generate emotion by expressing our own emotions (3.2.3 Complementary Opposites).

8. We can argue against the action that we actually prefer. When we take the opposing side, we are using what is known as reverse psychology. Since we are advocating giving us a reward, people know that we are only playing"devil's advocate,"representing the forces that want to deny us a reward. This works because when we push people, they will tend to push back (3.2.5 Dynamic Reversal).

Illustration:

Let us look at how all of these techniques are used to sell the most generic from of value in history, gold. (Full disclosure: as I write this, I have been invested in gold for quite some time, but I recently cut my position in half because of the amount of advertising out there).

1. We must target individuals from whom we want action. If we are running advertisement to sell gold, we run it on stations where people have money (Fox News, talk radio) not the stations where they don't (MTV, teeny-bop radio).

2. We must identify potential future events that create strong emotions in these people. Pitches for gold are based on economic uncertainty, specifically using the fear that people have of another stock market crash and inflation.

3. Individual emotional appeals can be specific. A financial consultant can get into an individual's specific worries based on their history in a way that a television commercial cannot.

4. Group emotional appeals can and should be more aggressive. Television commercials can be much louder, more aggressive, and broader in their claims. A financial consultant would lose credibility if he or she adopted a similar tone in real life.

5. We must use what is known about the past. "Gold has tripled in value over the last ten years."

6. We must use what is unknown about the future. "Experts predict that we could see it double and double again in the near future."

7. We must take the side of those from whom we want action. "I have invested in gold and you should too."

8. We can argue against the action that we actually prefer. "Investing in gold is not right for everyone."

On this last point, I am reminded of a good friend and salesperson, Keith Westphal, who would always challenge people about whether or not they could afford to make a given purchase. While qualification is part of the beginning of the sales process, to understand what a customer can afford, he would also use it at the end. When a customer would hesitate to make a decision at the end of the process, he would be sympathetic,"Though we both know this is what you want and need, many customers really cannot afford to make this investment and that is nothing to be embarrassed about."Challenged in this way, people would often make the purchase just to prove him wrong about their finances.

8.6.0 Winning Attention

Sun Tzu's eight key methods describing how to win the attention of others for our claims.

"You can speak, but you will not be heard.
You must use gongs and drums."
Sun Tzu's The Art of War 7:4:2-3

"Every interview is about showmanship. Every person who walks into an interview is operating at a level of showmanship. The only question is whether you are aware of it and whether you follow the principles of good showmanship."
Alan Fox

General Principle: Win the attention of others to get rewarded for claims.

Situation:

In today's increasingly crowded environment, more and more people are competing for attention. We need people to recognize us in order to reward us. We must get people's attention before we can get their support. If people are unaware of us, they cannot support us. People hear only what they want to hear. It requires work to get people to hear our claims. We must compete in an environment full of claims. This makes getting attention when we need it that much more difficult. Getting time with people is hard enough, but making an impression is even harder.

Opportunity:

The chaos of crowded, dynamic environments creates the desire for clarity and simplicity. Our opportunity arises from the nature of complementary opposites. No matter how crowded our environment is, there are always openings because there are always needs (3.1.4 Openings). As conditions change, we must continually adjust our communication to contrast it with conditions. In noisy environments, we speak quietly to get attention. In rooms that are "dead," we speak loudly and ask people to make noise to liven the situation up. In the dark, we use light. In the light, we use shadow. Any method of communication gets old and tired if it goes on too long. We have to change things up to keep it interesting.

Key Methods:

There are eight key methods describing Sun Tzu's principles for getting attention.

1. We win people's attention with change. When our positions are so new that they are unknown, we must excite curiosity and interest in others. If our positions are better known and taken for granted, we must accentuate the changes by making them entertaining. The message must suit changing conditions either by leveraging the change or playing against it (4.8 Climate Support).

2. We win people's attention by stimulating the senses. This means developing pictures, props, and gimmicks to get people's attention. Visual communication is more powerful than words. Movement is more interesting than stability. Strategy often requires a good dose of showmanship and magic. However, we cannot get a decision regarding a reward out of chaos. Showmanship in strategy has its own special principles (2.3.3 Likely Reactions).

3. To get attention, we must first clear people's minds. Our first job is to clear people's minds. People have a lot on their minds. While their minds are cluttered, their resistance to new information is high. We must jolt them strongly enough to draw their attention. Then their resistance fades. People want to be entertained and stimulated but we cannot do this if they are distracted by what is in their heads (2.1.4 Surprise).

4. To get attention, we must give people a focus point for their self interest. We must tailor all messages to individual self-interest. If we want to win people's attention. We must tie our contract together into a single whole. Each idea must lead back to a central point. The central point must address the changing nature of our needs. We must not offer novel concepts alone. We must tie them together with comfortable, familiar ideas. Every reason to make the decision we want must amplify a single, clear message about our shared mission (1.6.1 Shared Mission).

5. To get attention, our focus points must offer simplicity. We must send everyone a consistent message. We must keep any presentation organized so that we don't frustrate our listeners. If people get nervous or frustrated, we hold their attention. We must describe our position simply so everyone can understand and appreciate it. Subtleties are important in education, but when we are asking for a decision, they are confusing. We must offer our ideas and proposals in ways that the decisionmakers enjoy. The work we put into our presentation illustrates our desire to offer something valuable to our supporters (2.1.1 Information Limits).

6. To get attention, we must make systems and processes entertaining and memorable. We must provide mental models and analogies that clarify our ideas while making them entertaining. Memorable communication requires a touch of drama. Most changes in position are not dramatic in themselves. We can dramatize a new position and its value by creating a visual symbol for the change. Pictures, trophies, and other signs of change are remembered (2.2.2 Mental Models).

7. To get attention, we must make balance out the situation. We play it up when we are ignored, and play it down when we are hyped. We surprise people when we can be enthusiastic about the barriers to deciding. Friendliness, enthusiasm, and patience wear down any resistance. We are successful in getting rewarded if we focus on the needs of others (3.2.3 Complementary Opposites).

8. To get attention, we must wait for a response. When we ask for a decision regarding a reward, we must wait for the decision-maker to respond. If the reward is coming to us naturally, we must do nothing that gets in its way.We must stay friendly no matter what their initial answer. Decision-makers must offer objections to test the strength of our position (4.2 Choosing Non-Action).

Illustration:

Here, we should look at the master for getting attention in the media, Apple, especially since this is written on the day before the release of the iPad.

1. We win people's attention with change. Apple has a tradition of releasing only game changing products, products that not only do new things but are new things. Its started with the Apple computer, then the Mac, and continued with the the iPod, followed by the iPhone. Even its failure, like the Newton, attempted to be something new and different.

2. We win people's attention by stimulating the senses. Apple is a design company. It seeks to seduce the eyes and the other senses. It offers far and away the most sensual products, which is why it has done so well.

3. To get attention, we must first clear people's minds. The iPad isn't a new laptop. It seeks to replace the laptop in our thinking. Even before it was announced, the mystery was used to create an open space for something new to appear.

4. To get attention, we must give people a focus point for their self interest. Apple does this in a variety of ways, but the most interesting is the way the product appeals to ego and status. Apple customers gladly pay hundreds more for the first versions of new product simply so they can be the first to get attention from their friends and associates.

5. To get attention, our focus points must offer simplicity. All of Apple's designs are minimalistic, eliminating buttons and controls and, to a large degree, having to think about how things works. Some attack Apple for making simplicity so central to is product design.

6. To get attention, we must make systems and processes entertaining and memorable. Apple's product releases leverage the genius of others to promote its products, garnering appearances on Letterman and Colbert.

7. To get attention, we must make balance out the situation. Apple starts with secrecy, puts out a lot of information, and then goes back to that secrecy as people consume the available information and grow hungry for more. Apple always leaves questions that grow more important over time until it does its next product announcement.

8. To get attention, we must wait for a response. In Apple's case, this response is initially the consumption and growing hunger for more information. This is followed by the product release, which is always less than meets demand. Every step in the promotion cycle is designed to create desire rather than satisfaction.

8.7.0 Productivity Improvement

Sun Tzu's seven key methods for improving internal production to harvest rewards to support external competition.

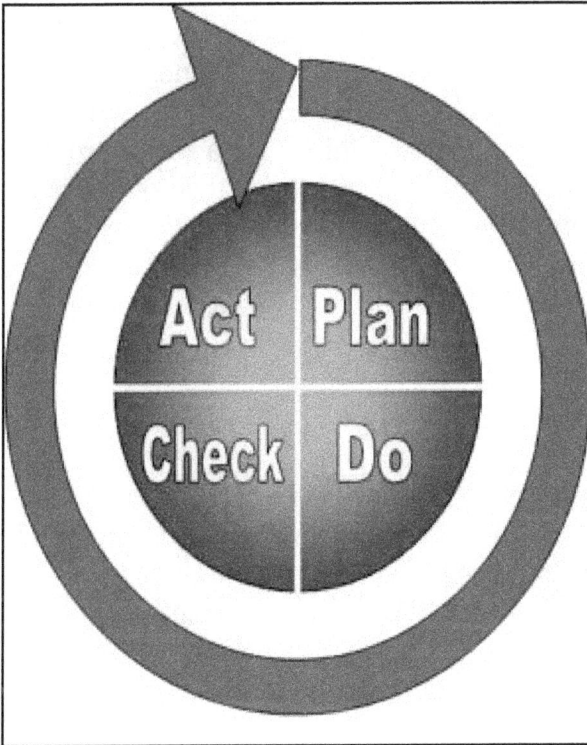

"You must master command.
The nation must support you."
Sun Tzu's The Art of War 3:4:1-2

"Without continual growth and progress, such words as improvement, achievement, and success have no meaning."
Benjamin Franklin

General Principle: We must continuously improve our control over our positions to give us more competitive resources.

Situation:

Our strategic positions have both an inside and an outside. The outside is the surface where our position makes contact with the competitive environment, the realm of strategy. The inside is our span of control, the realm of planning. Through planning and organization, we are able to improve our internal systems and make ourselves more productive within our span of control. The problem is that internal systems take on a life of their own. This problem only gets worse when strategic positions are successful, growing and expanding over time. As a position grows into an organization, its internal systems gradually become more and more isolated from the external environment.

Opportunity:

The easiest way to get more rewards from any existing position is to continually improve our control over it. Planning and organization can dramatically improve the productivity of a position over time. Since our only strategic goal is improving our position, the methods of production play a critical place in good strategy. The practice of continual improvement in particular has much in common with the adaptive loop of strategy (1.8.2 The Adaptive Loop). The differences between the two, however, are critical. Our opportunity is in understanding the differences between these two different loops and, most importantly, the feedback between them.

Key Methods:

The following seven key methods describe the continuous process by which we improve internal productivity.

1. Like competitive progress, productivity improvement is a loop. There are many different forms of the continuous improvement loop but we will discuss the general concept in terms of

Deming's PDCA cycle. This loop was popularized by the quality movement of the 1980's and is one of the best documented versions of the process. The PDCA loop intersects with the Progress Cycle of Listen->Aim->Move->Claim. The beginning and end of its loop start and end with our competitive mission. Its other steps reflect the steps of the Progress Cycle in interesting ways (1.8 Progress Cycle).

2. The productivity loop starts with a design step creating a specification of expected output. In Deming's terms, this is the *plan* stage. In the competitive loop, a general arises from our external mission, which is the core of a the progress cycle. In production, the more specific our goals, the better our internal control (1.9.2 Span of Control).

3. The productivity loop continues with the implementation of the new processes on as small a scale as possible. In Deming's cycle, this is the *do* stage. It is similar to the *move* step in the Progress Cycle and reflects many of its values, including minimizing mistakes by testing ideas in a small way. (5.4 Minimizing Action).

4. The productivity loop then measures the results of new processes against specification. Deming called this the *check* stage. In the process cycle, measurement and comparison comes at the end of the cycle, in the *claim* stage. Both steps compare the previous situation with the new one to determine the success of the change (1.3.1 Competitive Comparison).

5. The productivity loop ends with an analysis to determine any causes for failure. In Deming, this is the *act* stage. Since production processes are linear systems , the causes of problems can be identified by reductionism, breaking a system into its parts. This is the opposite from the way that we loop for opportunities in the *listen* and *aim* stage of the progress cycle, which requires us seeing the big picture (2.5 The Big Picture).

6. By using this productivity loop, we gradually improve the controlled processes through which we create products that we expect to have external value. Through the loop, we learn to eliminate efforts that do not contribute to the process. We learn to do less and less to produce more and more. These process create the additional resources we need in competition with others, since competition is always constrained by resources. (3.1.1 Resource Limitations).

7. *The productivity loop relies upon the competitive loop to provide external feedback*. In the end, the continuous improvement of production must be measured against external positioning. The PDCA only measures the efficiency of the internal system, but the internal system can only make products. The value of those products can only be measured externally. If we are not guided by external measure, we can fall into the trap of very efficient production that creates no real value. The most efficient internal process in the world are meaningless if their product is not valued outside the system itself (1.4 The External Environment).

Illustration:

We can illustrate these ideas with examples from business, but in all of these examples, we go back to the final rule, connecting internal production to external competition, since this is where this loop goes wrong.

1. *Like competitive progress, productivity improvement is a loop*. American car companies have all dramatically improved their internal processes over the last twenty years but that hasn't helped them economically. Their internal organization became more and more isolated from the external market. Since they simply improved the systems that produced cars that people didn't want to buy, they ended up going bankrupt.

2. *The productivity loop starts with a design step creating a specification of expected output*. The product specified must be one people want. Today's leader in retail, Wal-Mart, has developed an extraordinarily efficient distribution system in the pursuit of low prices, low prices alone do not determine value. Retailers have to offer what people want. The previous retail leader in low-prices, KMart, went out of business because nobody wanted what they sold. Retail history is strewn with bankruptcies as leading retailers end up selling the wrong products for the wrong reasons.

3. The productivity loop continues with the implementation of the new processes on as small a scale as possible. You can see the difference in the scale of internal testing by comparing manufacturing cars with selling retail products. Test of distribution for any product can be performed on a very small, affordable scale. In manufactuing, we can safely make small changes to improve the production of an existing car, but the creation of a new car requires a substantial investment even at the smallest scale. Yet it is the new car rather than the existing one that requires external testing to verify its value.

4. The productivity loop then measures the results of new processes against specification. Whether you are manufacturing a car or selling retail products, there is a difference between an internal test of process and an external test of value. A manufacturing or distribution test, only tests the internal efficiency of the process.

5. The productivity loop ends with an analysis to determine any causes for failure. Plans for manufacturing and distribution that work on paper often do not work in reality. This is true even for the controlled environment of the factory or the distribution system. However, because information is both more available and less dynamic in a controlled environment, we can get a fix on causes and control them.

6. The productivity loop relies upon the competitive loop to provide external feedback. In business, the control of the internal by the external is called "market discipline." Continuous improvement has dramatically improve the quality of products and the efficiency of production processes for everyone as more people master these methods. But while more efficient production makes us more competitive, competitive success requires more than improving production methods.

7. By using this productivity loop, we gradually improve the controlled processes through which we create products that we expect to have external value. Let us end with an illustration that is not from business, but from our personal relationships. We can continually improve our relationships by working on improving ourselves through this productivity loop. For example, we can work at eliminating our bad habits. However, the more we focus on ourselves in our relationships, the less happy the relationship as a whole can be. Relationships produce value but unlike making products, there is no such thing as a more efficient personal relationship.

8.7.1 Position Erosion

Sun Tzu's eight key methods for gauging the erosion of our current positions.

> *"Positions turn around.*
> *Nevertheless, you must never be defeated."*
>> Sun Tzu's The Art of War 5:4:5-6

> *"I know of no more encouraging fact than the*
> *unquestioning ability of man to evaluate his life by a*
> *conscious endeavor."*
>> Henry David Thoreau

General Principle: We must continuously improve our control over our positions to give us more competitive resources.

Situation:

Positions erode slowly. It is easy to take our positions for granted. We tend to over-value exiting positions as they decline over time. We base our judgments upon the past. We find it difficult to see a gradual decline. We defend an existing position simply because it is ours. As a position declines, we continue to investing in its maintenance even when it is no longer returning meaningful rewards. Past success doesn't mean future success, but the more successful a position has been in the past, the more we tend to invest in it whether those investment pay off or not.

Opportunity:

We must always have new goals. No matter how far we progress in life, we can envision a better position. Few of us are so comfortable that we do not desire more. At the very least, all of us desire to hold onto what we have. Positions can improve automatically if the climate improves even if the tendency is for them to degrade over time. All positions have advantages and disadvantages. We use the advantages of our position to reap its rewards. Our current balance of costs and rewards provides a valuable tool for evaluating whether we can maintain our position or if we must advance it.

Key Methods:

The following eight key methods explain how we recognize when our position is eroding.

1. If we do nothing to improve our position, we should expect it to degrade over time. Though improving conditions can automatically improve our position, the typical situation is that a static position is increasingly inappropriate to conditions (1.1.1 Position Dynamics).

2. If our position seems static, we should assume it is declining. Many changes in conditions that erode a position happen below the surface. A situation that looks static is probably declining without our seeing it (1.1.2 Defending Positions).

3. All progress in developing an existing position reaches a point of diminishing returns. When we work to continuously improve our existing position, we will reap more rewards. This means that we have to continually re-evaluate every part of our position (8.7 Productivity Improvement).

4. To evaluate the erosion of our position, we must use an objective form of measurement. If easily measured rewards (such as money) are not available, use the positive event/investment event measurement system (8.3.1 Gauging Value).

5. To evaluate the erosion of our position, we must track investments in maintaining or improving it over time. Physically recorded measurements are more reliable than mentally recorded ones, but not always practical. Minimally, we should have an idea of frequency of investment (1.8.3 Cycle Time).

6. To evaluate the erosion of our position, we must track its rewards over time. Physical measurements are better but the frequency of rewards is an easier and more universal measure (8.1.3 Reward Timing).

7. To evaluate the erosion of our position, we must know the trend of an existing position. If our position is improving or declining, we should know it. We should also have a sense for how quickly it is improving and declining and the change in relationship between investment and rewards (1.3.1 Competitive Comparison).

8. As our position is declining, the urgency of advancing it increases. We need to work to find new opportunities to change the trend. (3.0 Identifying Opportunities.

Illustration:

These key methods are interesting because they apply to every aspect of our lives.

1. If we do nothing to improve our position, we should expect it to degrade over tim*e.* Our lives are made of many different positions: positions in relationships, positions at our work, positions in our health, etc.

2. *If our position seems static, we should assume it is declining*. If our careers, our romantic relationships, oru health, and so on seem static, they are really getting worse without our recognizing it.

3. *All progress in developing an existing position reaches a point of diminishing returns.* In selling, we should known if we are making progress or losing ground with each prospect, even before there are sales to record. We should track our positive calls versus no progress calls both for each prospect and for our sales day as a whole. A positive increase in this trend shows we are improving our position when we have no other measure.

4. *To evaluate the erosion of our position, we must use an objective form of measurement*. Perhaps the hardest positions to evaluate are our personal ones. In our relationships, we should known if we are making progress or losing ground in each of our important sales relationships. We should have a sense of our number of enjoyable shared experiences over time so we know when our relationships are being kept alive or not. A positive increase in this trend shows we are improving our relationships.

5. *To evaluate the erosion of our position, we must track investments in maintaining or improving it over time*. In our health, we should known if we are making progress or losing ground in our investment in our physical condition. When we are younger, we take our health for granted,

6. maintaining it without seeming to have to make an investment. Our weight is a useful generic measure of health, but the frequency and length of our exercise is important. As we gradually become less physically active in our daily lives, we must replace that activity with purposeful exercise, increasing it rather than decreasing it as we get older.

7. *To evaluate the erosion of our position, we must track its rewards over time*. We should have an idea of the direction of all of these positions over time. Reward in business or selling are easily measured in dollars. Rewards in relationships and health are harder to track but even more real. Even as we age, our health can become more robust if we stop taking health for granted and start working on our health daily. Our relationships can grow deeper over time, but again, only if we work at them.

8. *To evaluate the erosion of our position, we must know the trend of an existing position.* All well-run businesses have income statements that compare their current sales and expenses to the past so they can see the trend. This idea simply expands this same concept of accounting to a wider variety of situations.

9. *As our position is declining, the urgency of advancing it increases.* When we grow stagnant, we must look more intensely for new areas in which to advance in both our professional and personal lives.

8.7.2 Abandoning Positions

Sun Tzu's six key methods describing how we abandon a losing position safely.

*"If you are defeated, you can recover.
You must use the four seasons correctly."*
                      Sun Tzu's The Art of War 5:2:9-10

"Come on, come on and there'll be no turning back. You were only killing time and it'll kill you right back."
Jim Steinem's "Out Of The Frying Pan (And Into The Fire)"

General Principle: We must establish new positions quickly but leave existing position as slowly as possible.

Situation:

More frequently than we would like, we must abandon a losing position. Abadoning a position is difficult because our strategic position gives us all our resources. A losing position is not just a position that costs more to win than it is worth. It is any position that costs more to maintain that it is worth. It must be abandoned, but, as is so often the case, the biggest danger in abandoning a losing position is overreacting. A bad situation can always be made worse by not handling it correctly. When we are in a losing position, it is all too easy to jump out of the frying pan and into the fire.

Opportunity:

The need to abandon a bad position must be viewed as an opportunity. The worse a position is, the more easily it can be improved. When we hit bottom, every direction is up. Though we cannot magically turn a bad position into a great position overnight, we can safely abandon losing positions for better ones if we know the secrets. We must minimize our mistakes (5.0 Minimizing Mistakes). We can then find a way out by using the uncertainty of the environment (5.2.1 Choosing Adaptability), the inevitable up and down cycles of conditions (1.4.1 Climate Shift) and the natural balance of strength and weakness (3.5 Strength and Weakness).

Key Methods:

The following six key methods describe what we must do to abandon a failing position safely.

1. To abandon a losing position, we must first focus on the big picture. We must understand the conditions surrounding our position. We must understand the surrounding conditions to find the direction in which we can move the most safely (2.5 The Big Picture).

2. To abandon a losing position, we must keep our move a secret by avoiding meeting opponents. We never want to meet opposition when we are in a losing position. If opponents know we are in a losing position, they will come after us, so we must keep our situation a secret, even from our contact network (2.7 Information Secrecy).

3. To abandon a losing position, we must consider its holding power. Even a losing situation can temporarily be better than the alternatives. Moving from a position has its own costs. These costs are associated by what we call the"holding power"of the position. The extremes of holding power are"sticky"and"slippery"positions. Sticky positions cannot be abandoned without preparing to pass through an even worse position. Slippery one positions are disastrous if we leave them in the wrong direction. Before we move, we must know how to handle these problems of holding power correctly (4.5.3 Surface Holding Power).

4. To abandon a losing position, we must determine the nature of climate shift. There is a difference between being in the down part of a cycle and in a long-term downward trend. A cycle will return, at least temporarily. If we are in a cycle, we should move when the cycle improves, temporarily giving us more resources. If we are in a trend, we must find a way to get on the opposite side of that trend as quickly as possible, using the methods of reversal (3.2.5 Dynamic Reversal).

5. To abandon a losing position, we must find what is the most valuable in our knowledge about our position. The issue is always how we can get the most value out of a position. The primary value of every position is the knowledge that it gives us. Our position's unique perspective can give us insight that can be valuable to others. Experience from a losing position can create value simply by helping others avoid similar mistakes (1.6.1 Shared Mission).

6. To abandon a losing position, we must establish alternative positions quickly but leave the existing position as slowly as we can afford. The general rule is that it is best to take new positions quickly but leave existing position slowly. We cannot afford to panic in any case, but the speed with which we move must be determined by whether position is suffering from a slow bleed or from a gushing artery. (5.6 Defensive Advances)

Illustration:

Let us illustrate these principles drawing from many different competitive arenas

1. To abandon a losing position, we must first focus on the big picture. If we are having problems in our career, we must determine whether the source of the problem is our company, our industry, our profession, or in ourselves.

2. To abandon a losing position, we must keep our move a secret by avoiding meeting opponents. If we find out our company is on the verge of laying people off, we must keep that a secret from everyone else at work or else we will compete with them in our job search.

3. To abandon a losing position, we must consider its holding power. A marketing agreement can prove to be costly, but abandoning that agreement can even be more costly if it generates lawsuits and makes future marketing agreement with anyone less likely.

4. To abandon a losing position, we must determine the nature of climate shift. If we are out of work as a computer programmer in today's market, we do not have to find a new career. If we are out of work as a assembly line worker, we do.

5. To abandon a losing position, we must find what is the most valuable in our knowledge about our position. If we get into trouble borrowing money, there is value in our knowledge in helping others avoid that problem.

6. To abandon a losing position, we must establish alternative positions quickly but leave the existing position as slowly as we can afford. Like rock climbing, we cling to our current hold until we are certain of our next hold, but if our current hold is crumbling , we may have to trust to fate and jump.

Glossary of Key Concepts

This glossary is keyed to the most common English words used in the translation of *The Art of War*. Those terms only capture the strategic concepts generally. Though translated as English nouns, verbs, adverbs, or adjectives, the Chinese characters on which they are based are totally conceptual, not parts of speech. For example, the character for conflict is translated as the noun "conflict," as the verb "fight," and as the adjective "disputed." Ancient written Chinese was a conceptual language, not a spoken one. More like mathematical terms, these concepts are primarily defined by the strict structure of their relationships with other concepts. The Chinese names shown in parentheses with the characters are primarily based on Pinyin, but we occasionally use Cantonese terms to make each term unique.

Advance (*Jeun* 進): to move into new **ground**; to expand your **position**; to move forward in a campaign; the opposite of **flee**.

Advantage, *benefit* (*Li* 利): an opportunity arising from having a better **position** relative to an **enemy**; an opening left by an **enemy**; a **strength** that matches against an **enemy's weakness**; where fullness meets emptiness; a desirable characteristic of a strategic **position**.

Aim, *vision, foresee* (*Jian* 見): **focus** on a specific **advantage**, opening, or opportunity; predicting movements of an **enemy**; a skill of a **leader** in observing **climate**.

Analysis, *plan* (*Gai* 計): a comparison of relative **position**; the examination of the five factors that define a strategic **position**; a combination of **knowledge** and **vision**; the ability to see through **deception**.

Army: see **war**.

Attack, *invade* (*Gong* 攻): a movement to new **ground**; advancing a strategic **position**; action against an **enemy** in the sense of moving into his **ground**; opposite of **defend**; does not necessarily mean **conflict**.

Bad, *ruined* (*Pi* 圮): a condition of the **ground** that makes **advance** difficult; destroyed; terrain that is broken and difficult to traverse; one of the nine situations or types of terrain.

Barricaded: see **obstacles**.

Battle (*Zhan* 戰): to challenge; to engage an **enemy**; generically, to meet a challenge; to choose a confrontation with an **enemy** at a specific time and place; to focus all your resources on a task; to establish superiority in a **position**; to challenge an **enemy** to increase **chaos**; that which is **controlled** by **surprise**; one of the four forms of **attack**; the response to a **desperate situation**; character meaning was originally "big meeting," though later took on the meaning "big weapon"; not necessarily **conflict**.

Bravery, *courage* (<u>Yong</u> 勇): the ability to face difficult choices; the character quality that deals with the changes of **CLIMATE;** courage of conviction; willingness to act on vision; one of the six characteristics of a leader.

Break, *broken*, *divided* (<u>Po</u> 破): to **divide** what is **complete**; the absence of a **uniting philosophy**; the opposite of <u>unity</u>.

Calculate, *count* (<u>Shu</u> 数): mathematical comparison of quantities and qualities; a measurement of **distance** or troop size.

Change, *transform* (<u>Bian</u> 變): transition from one **condition** to another; the ability to adapt to different situations; a natural characteristic of **climate**.

Chaos, *disorder* (<u>Juan</u> 亂): **conditions** that cannot be **foreseen**; the natural state of confusion arising from **battle**; one of six weaknesses of an organization; the opposite of **control**.

Claim, *position*, *form* (<u>Xing</u> 形): to use the **ground**; a shape or specific condition of **ground**; the **ground** that you **control**; to use the benefits of the **ground**; the formations of troops; one of the four key skills in making progress.

Climate, *heaven* (<u>Tian</u> 天): the passage of time; the realm of uncontrollable **change**; divine providence; the weather; trends that **change** over time; generally, the future; what one must **aim** at in the future; one of five key factors in **analysis;** the opposite of **ground**.

Command (<u>Ling</u> 令): to order or the act of ordering subordinates; the decisions of a **leader**; the creation of **methods**.

Competition: see <u>war.</u>

Complete: see <u>unity.</u>

Condition: see **ground**.

Confined, *surround* (<u>Wei</u> 圍): to encircle; a **situation** or **stage** in which your options are limited; the proper tactic for dealing with an **enemy** that is ten times smaller; to seal off a smaller **enemy**; the characteristic of a **stage** in which a larger **force** can be attacked by a smaller one; one of nine **situations** or **stages**.

Conflict, *fight* (<u>Zheng</u> 爭): to contend; to dispute; direct confrontation of arms with an **enemy**; highly desirable **ground** that creates disputes; one of nine types of **ground,** terrain, or stages.

Constricted, *narrow* (<u>Ai</u> 狹): a confined space or niche; one of six field positions; the limited extreme of the dimension distance; the opposite of **spread-out**.

Control, *govern* (<u>Chi</u> 治): to manage situations; to overcome disorder; the opposite of **chaos**.

Dangerous: see **serious**.

Dangers, *adverse* (Ak 阨): a condition that makes it difficult to **advance**; one of three dimensions used to evaluate advantages; the dimension with the extreme field **positions** of **entangling** and **supporting**.

Death, *desperate* (_Si_ 死): to end or the end of life or efforts; an extreme situation in which the only option is **battle**; one of nine **stages** or types of **terrain**; one of five types of **spies**; opposite of **survive**.

Deception, *bluffing, illusion* (_Gui_ 詭):
to control perceptions; to control information; to mislead an **enemy**; an attack on an opponent's **aim**; the characteristic of war that confuses perceptions.

Defend (_Shou_ 守): to guard or to hold a **ground**; to remain in a **position**; the opposite of **attack**.

Detour (_Yu_ 迂): the indirect or unsuspected path to a **position**; the more difficult path to **advantage**; the route that is not **direct**.

Direct, *straight* (_Jik_ 直): a straight or obvious path to a goal; opposite of **detour**.

Distance, *distant* (_Yuan_ 遠): the space separating **ground**; to be remote from the current location; to occupy **positions** that are not close to one another; one of six field positions; one of the three dimensions for evaluating opportunities; the emptiness of space.

Divide, *separate* (_Fen_ 分): to break apart a larger force; to separate from a larger group; the opposite of **join** and **focus**.

Double agent, *reverse* (_Fan_ 反): to turn around in direction; to change a situation; to switch a person's allegiance; one of five types of spies.

Easy, *light* (_Qing_ 輕): to require little effort; a **situation** that requires little effort; one of nine **stages** or types of terrain; opposite of **serious**.

Emotion, *feeling* (_Xin_ 心): an unthinking reaction to **aim**, a necessary element to inspire **moves**; a component of esprit de corps; never a sufficient cause for **attack**.

Enemy, *competitor* (_Dik_ 敵): one who makes the same **claim**; one with a similar **goal**; one with whom comparisons of capabilities are made.

Entangling, *hanging* (_Gua_ 懸): a **position** that cannot be returned to; any **condition** that leaves no easy place to go; one of six field positions.

Evade, *avoid* (_Bi_ 避): the tactic used by small competitors when facing large opponents.

Fall apart, *collapse* (_Beng_ 崩): to fail to execute good decisions; to fail to use a **constricted position**; one of six weaknesses of an organization.

Fall down, *sink* (_Haam_ 陷): to fail to make good decisions; to **move** from a **supporting position**; one of six weaknesses of organizations.

Feelings, *affection, love* (_Ching_ 情): the bonds of relationship; the result of a shared **philosophy**; requires management.

Fight, *struggle* (Dou 鬥): to engage in **conflict**; to face difficulties.

Fire (*Huo* 火): an environmental weapon; a universal analogy for all weapons.

Flee, *retreat, northward* (*Bei* 北) :to abandon a **position**; to surrender **ground**; one of six weaknesses of an **army**; opposite of **advance**.

Focus, *concentrate* (*Zhuan* 專): to bring resources together at a given time; to **unite** forces for a purpose; an attribute of having a shared **philosophy**; the opposite of *divide*.

Force (*Lei* 力): power in the simplest sense; a **group** of people bound by **unity** and **focus**; the relative balance of **strength** in opposition to **weakness**.

Foresee: see **aim**.

Fullness: see **strength**.

General: see **leader**.

Goal: see **philosophy**.

Ground, *situation, stage* (*Di* 地): the earth; a specific place; a specific condition; the place one competes; the prize of competition; one of five key factors in competitive analysis; the opposite of **climate**.

Groups, *troops* (*Dui* 隊): a number of people united under a shared **philosophy**; human resources of an organization; one of the five targets of fire attacks.

Inside, *internal* (*Nei* 内): within a **territory** or organization; an insider; one of five types of spies; opposite of *Wai*, outside.

Intersecting, *highway* (*Qu* 衢): a **situation** or **ground** that allows you to **join**; one of nine types of terrain.

Join (*Hap* 合): to unite; to make allies; to create a larger **force**; opposite of **divide**.

Knowledge, *listening* (*Zhi*: 知): to have information; the result of listening; the first step in advancing a **position**; the basis of strategy.

Lax, *loosen* (*Shii* 弛): too easygoing; lacking discipline; one of six weaknesses of an army.

Leader, *general, commander* (*Jiang* 將): the decision-maker in a competitive unit; one who **listens** and **aims**; one who manages **troops**; superior of officers and men; one of the five key factors in analysis; the conceptual opposite of *fa*, the established methods, which do not require decisions.

Learn, *compare* (*Xiao* 效): to evaluate the relative qualities of **enemies**.

Listen, *obey* (*Ting* 聽): to gather **knowledge**; part of **analysis**.

Listening: see **knowledge**.

Local, *countryside* (_Xiang_ 鄉): the nearby **ground**; to have **knowledge** of a specific **ground**; one of five types of **spies**.

Marsh (_Ze_ 澤): **ground** where footing is unstable; one of the four types of **ground**; analogy for uncertain situations.

Method: see **system**.

Mission: see **philosophy**.

Momentum, *influence* (_Shi_ 勢): the **force** created by **surprise** set up by **standards;** used with **timing**.

Mountains, *hill, peak* (_Shan_ 山): uneven **ground**; one of four types of **ground**; an analogy for all unequal **situations**.

Move, *march, act* (_Hang_ 行): action toward a position or goal; used as a near synonym for <u>dong</u>, act.

Nation (_Guo_ 國): the state; the productive part of an organization; the seat of political power; the entity that controls an **army** or competitive part of the organization.

Obstacles, *barricaded* (_Xian_ 險): to have barriers; one of the three characteristics of the **ground**; one of six field positions; as a field position, opposite of **unobstructed**.

Open, *meeting, crossing* (_Jiao_ 來): to share the same **ground** without conflict; to come together; a **situation** that encourages a race; one of nine **terrains** or **stages**.

Opportunity: see <u>advantage.</u>

Outmaneuver (_Sou_ 走): to go astray; to be **forced** into a **weak position**; one of six weaknesses of an army.

Outside, *external* (_Wai_ 外): not within a **territory** or **army**; one who has a different perspective; one who offers an objective view; opposite of **internal**.

Philosophy, *mission, goals* (_Tao_ 道): the shared **goals** that **unite** an **army**; a system of thought; a shared viewpoint; literally "the way"; a way to work together; one of the five key factors in **analysis**.

Plateau (_Liu_ 陸): a type of **ground** without defects; an analogy for any equal, solid, and certain **situation**; the best place for competition; one of the four types of **ground**.

Resources, *provisions* (_Liang_ 糧): necessary supplies, most commonly food; one of the five targets of fire attacks.

Restraint: see **timing.**

Reward, *treasure, money* (_Bao_ 賞): profit; wealth; the necessary compensation for competition; a necessary ingredient for **victory**; **victory** must pay.

Scatter, *dissipating* (_San_ 散): to disperse; to lose **unity**; the pursuit of separate **goals** as opposed to a central **mission**; a situation that causes a **force** to scatter; one of nine conditions or types of terrain.

Serious, *heavy* (_Chong_ 重): any task requiring effort and skill; a **situation** where resources are running low when you are deeply committed to a campaign or heavily invested in a project; a situation where opposition within an organization mounts; one of nine **stages** or types of **terrain**.

Siege (_Gong Cheng_ 攻城): to move against entrenched positions; any movement against an **enemy's strength**; literally "strike city"; one of the four forms of attack; the least desirable form of attack.

Situation: see **ground.**

Speed, *hurry* (Sai 馳): to **move** over **ground** quickly; the ability to **advance positions** in a minimum of time; needed to take advantage of a window of opportunity.

Spread-out, *wide* (_Guang_ 廣): a surplus of **distance**; one of the six **ground positions**; opposite of **constricted.**

Spy, *conduit, go-between* (_Gaan_ 間): a source of information; a channel of communication; literally, an "opening between."

Stage: see **ground.**

Standard, *proper, correct* (_Jang_ 正): the expected behavior; the standard approach; proven methods; the opposite of surprise; together with **surprise** creates **momentum.**

Storehouse, *house* (_Ku_ 庫): a place where resources are stockpiled; one of the five targets for fire attacks.

Stores, *accumulate, savings* (_Ji_ 糧):resources that have been stored; any type of inventory; one of the five targets of fire attacks.

Strength, *fullness, satisfaction* (_Sat_ 壹): wealth or abundance or resources; the state of being crowded; the opposite of Xu, empty.

Supply wagons, *transport* (_Zi_ 輜): the movement of **resources** through **distance**; one of the five targets of fire attacks.

Support, *supporting* (_Zhii_ 支): to prop up; to enhance; a **ground position** that you cannot leave without losing **strength**; one of six field positions; the opposite extreme of gua, entangling.

Surprise, *unusual, strange* (_Qi_ 奇) : the unexpected; the innovative; the opposite of **standard**; together with **standards** creates **momentum**.

Surround: see **confined**.

Survive, *live, birth* (*Shaang* 生): the state of being created, started, or beginning; the state of living or surviving; a temporary condition of fullness; one of five types of spies; the opposite of **death**.

System, *method* (*Fa* 法): a set of procedures; a group of techniques; steps to accomplish a **goal**; one of the five key factors in analysis; the realm of groups who must follow procedures; the opposite of the **leader**.

Territory, *terrain*: see **ground**.

Timing, *restraint* (*Jie* 節): to withhold action until the proper time; to release tension; a companion concept to **momentum**.

Troops: see **group**.

Unity, *whole, oneness* (*Yi* 一): the characteristic of a **group** that shares a **philosophy**; the lowest number; a **group** that acts as a unit; the opposite of **divided**.

Unobstructed, *expert* (*Tong* 通): without obstacles or barriers; **ground** that allows easy movement; open to new ideas; one of six field positions; opposite of **obstructed**.

Victory, *win, winning* (*Sing* 勝): success in an endeavor; getting a reward; serving your mission; an event that produces more than it consumes; to make a profit.

War, *competition, army* (**Bing** 兵): a dynamic situation in which **positions** can be won or lost; a contest in which a **reward** can be won; the conditions under which the principles of strategy work.

Water, *river* (*Shui* 水): a fast-changing **ground**; fluid **conditions**; one of four types of **ground**; an analogy for change.

Weakness, *emptiness, need* (*Xu* 虛): the absence of people or resources; devoid of **force**; the point of **attack** for an **advantage**; a characteristic of **ground** that enables **speed**; poor; the opposite of strength.

Win, *winning*: see **victory**.

Wind, *fashion, custom* (*Feng* 風): the pressure of environmental forces.

The *Art of War Playbook* Series

There are over two-hundred and thirty articles on Sun Tzu's competitive principles in the nine volumes of the *Art of War Playbook*. Each volume covers a specific area of Sun Tzu strategy.

VOLUME ONE: - POSITIONS

VOLUME TWO: -PERSPECTIVE

VOLUME THREE: - OPPORTUNITIES

VOLUME FOUR: - PROBABILITY

VOLUME FIVE: - MISTAKES

VOLUME SIX: - SITUATIONS

VOLUME SEVEN: - MOMENTUM

VOLUME EIGHT: - REWARDS

VOLUME NINE: - VULNERABILITIES.

About the Translator and Author

Gary Gagliardi is recognized as America's leading expert on Sun Tzu's *The Art of War*. An award-winning author and business strategist, his many books on Sun Tzu's strategy have been translated around the world. He has appeared on hundreds of talk shows nationwide, providing strategic insight on the breaking news. He has trained decision makers from some of the world's most successful organizations in competitive thinking. His workshops convert Sun Tzu's many principles into a series of practical tools for handling common competitive challenges.

Gary began using Sun Tzu's competitive principles in a successful corporate career and when he started his own software company. In 1990, he wrote his first *Art of War* adaptation for his company's salespeople. By 1992, his company was on *Inc. Magazine's* list of the 500 fastest-growing privately held companies in America. He personally won the U.S. Chamber of Commerce Blue Chip Quality Award and was an Ernst and Young Entrepreneur of the Year finalist. His customers—AT&T, GE, and Motorola, among others—began inviting him to speak at their conferences. After becoming a multimillionaire when he sold his software company in 1997, he continued teaching *The Art of War* around the world.

Gary has authored several breakthrough works on *The Art of War*. Ten of his books on strategy have won book award recognition in nine different non-fiction categories.

Art of War Books by Gary Gagliardi

Gary Gagliardi's Books are Available at:

SunTzus.com
Amazon.com
BarnesAndNoble.com
Itunes.apple.com

www.ingramcontent.com/pod-product-compliance
Lightning Source LLC
Chambersburg PA
CBHW071214200326
41519CB00018B/5515